Birdwatch

Birdwatch
TONY SOPER

Illustrations by
Robert Gillmor

Webb & Bower
EXETER, ENGLAND

First published in Great Britain 1982 by
Webb & Bower (Publishers) Limited
9 Colleton Crescent, Exeter, Devon EX2 4BY

This paperback edition
published 1985

Production Nick Facer

Designed by Peter Wrigley

Picture research by Anne-Marie Ehrlich

Copyright © Webb & Bower (Publishers) Limited 1982

British Library Cataloguing in Publication Data

Soper, Tony
  Tony Soper's birdwatch.
  1. Birds
  I. Title
  598   QL673

ISBN 0–86350–076–5

Typeset in Great Britain
by Keyspools Limited, Golborne, Lancashire

Printed and bound in Italy
by New Interlitho SpA

Contents

1
Introduction

Blue tit carrying food to nestlings.

More people belong to societies devoted to birds than to societies devoted to mammals. This may appear to be an extraordinary state of affairs. As mammals ourselves, our first interest outside our own species should perhaps be in those most closely related to us and, to some extent, this is the case. Zoos are visited mainly because of their mammal exhibits: elephants, giraffes, apes and seals attract more popular interest than the birds. On television programmes, mammals more than hold their own, once due allowance has been made for the relative difficulty of filming them in the wild. But in real life, in terms of face-to-face interest in wild creatures in the field, birds and birdwatchers are number one.

This is partly because birds are simply more accessible than mammals. Most of our mammals are nocturnal, pursuing a lifestyle which makes a virtue of avoiding human contact. Many people go through life without seeing a wild badger, or a shrew for that matter, oblivious of the fact that they are close neighbours. On the other hand, it would be difficult for the most desk-bound city executive to avoid noticing birds, even if the relationship is limited to irritation at an un-solicited dropping on his proudly polished car or the raucous courtship of seaside gulls.

Mammals further distance themselves from us by inhabiting an alien world of smell rather than sight. Reptiles and amphibians find few admirers, for complex and mostly ill-conceived reasons. Fish and fishy creatures, too, suffer the unfortunate tag 'cold-blooded' and clearly live in a different world.

These are all negative reasons for liking birds but there are many positive ones also. You can *see* birds, out in the open, enjoying the daylight as we do. They live in a world of sound, vision and movement, using much the same set of senses as we use ourselves. In the varied scenery and moderate climate of Britain, we are blessed with an abundance of both numbers and species. We share many characteristics and activities, apart from walking on two feet. We both make plentiful and varied use of our voices, all the way from fishwife scolding to the crooning of love. We also make much use of formal gestures and dances in our everyday relationships. We both build houses, using local materials and intricate construction techniques. There are many parallels in the whole business of family life, from courtship through care of a young family to adolescent dispersal. Other classes of animals do all of these things, each in their own way. Fish, too, indulge in elaborate courtship displays, build nests and care tenderly for their offspring but they might as well do it on the moon for all we see of the procedure. Birds, on the other hand, we can see going about their business. They are discreet but not too discreet. If we choose to show interest in their affairs, then it is no more than we do with our own close relations and friends.

While it is true that many birds much prefer to be left in peace, there is an astonishing list of those which display a touching willingness to be our neighbours. Swallows choose to live in our outhouses and martins under our eaves. Residents like robins and sparrows may regard your property as their own, with just as much title to it, what's more, in biological law.

Perhaps the most significant factor in our enjoyment of birds is their power of flight. There is more than a touch of envy in that enjoyment. How splendid it would be if we could climb effortlessly into the sky like a lark, to view the country round about! How convenient to take off for a season in the sun, when days shorten and nights are chill! Birds seem able always to go where the living is good. Reality is less rosy, of course, but flight appears no less wonderful. It has given birds the chance to diversify and conquer the world. Arctic terns pole-hop from the top of the globe to the bottom, enjoying a life of almost perpetual daylight. From the polar regions to the seemingly barren deserts, from the highest Himalayan peaks to the heart of the jungle and into the sea itself, from the caverns within the earth to the industrial wastelands and city centres, there are birds taking advantage of opportunities and looking for new ones. In sober truth, birds are not quite every-where; they do not penetrate far underground or far below the surface of the sea but they explore caves and dive underwater to much the same extent as people do—yet more in common.

Birds come in all shapes, sizes and lifestyles. Most hunt by day, only a few by night. Some are vegetarian, some are carnivores, some eat any-thing they can get hold of, including other birds. Some walk after their food, some hop, some fly, some swim or dive for it. Each is specially equipped for its job. One way or another, anything which grows gets eaten. Fruits, nuts, seeds, leaves, living creatures and decaying matter, all are grist to someone's mill.

Very roughly, we may divide birds into four categories according to the shape of their beaks: the hard-billed birds like sparrows or finches,

which have nutcracker beaks; the soft-billed birds like robins, which deal with insects; the dual-purpose bills, which take on anything; and the hook-billed birds of prey. Putting a name to these birds as you see them is a satisfying form of hunting in itself but there is more to birdwatching than that and nothing ever remains the same for long. The list of birds which ornithology admits to be British is in a continual state of flux. Species come and species go. Twenty-five years ago, hardly anyone had even heard of the collared dove *Streptopelia decaocto*. Now it has spread, in numbers, to every county throughout the British Isles. A hundred and fifty years ago, in my own county of Devon, starlings were winter visitors and the very occasional breeding pair were welcomed as a pleasure and a joy. Now it is fashionable to decry them as noisy bullies. Thus birds and birdwatching can offer an inexhaustibly interesting study. Their populations and their variety are dynamic; there will always be something new to explore in their relationship with each other and with us.

The highest bird density in the United Kingdom

Slapton Ley, South Devon. Coastal lagoons offer all-year-round birdwatching. Passage migrants flock through in spring and autumn, warblers build nests in the tall reeds in summer and the open water provides safe roosting for winter wildfowl.

is associated with suburbia. It has been estimated that suburban gardens support an average of thirty birds to the acre, a figure which exceeds that of the woodland habitat from which most of the birds originally came. Since many of us live in a habitat that clearly suits birds, it makes sense to give them extra encouragement and in so doing give ourselves a great deal of pleasure.

There are plenty of ways of influencing birds to share their lives with us. The first step is to provide food, in the shape of berry-bearing shrubs and trees or seed-producing plants or food scraps on the bird table. The second step is to provide nest places, whether natural ones in trees and hedges or artificial ones in nestboxes. Some mock-purists may say that it is wrong to interfere with the food and shelter of wild birds. But this is to perpetuate the long-standing nonsense that man is set apart from animals as a sort of superior being. As the

9

dominant animal, for the moment at least, it is clearly our job to exercise responsibility in our community, in its largest sense. In everything we do, we 'interfere' in the natural course of events, sometimes with disastrous results, sometimes with happy ones. Conservationists aim to manage things in such a way that we use our resources intelligently to the benefit of all.

Birds play their part in Earth's system, as agents of plant dispersal, pollination, pest control and as a primary food source serving man as well as many other creatures. In addition to their practical virtues, they provide us with a never-ending spectacle of beauty in colour, movement and song. Since pre-history, men have regarded birds with a powerful mixture of greed, pleasure and envy. In superstitious times, they were a rich source of omens. Ravens represented the Prince of Darkness; goldfinches, with their blood-marked faces and their predilection for thorns and thistles, symbolized Christ's Passion. An era of wholesale slaughter arrived with the development of accurate guns. Scientists themselves regarded it as essential that any specimen should be shot before it could be admitted to the List. Their interest lay in classification, achieved by the study of a collection of skins. The curious mix of part scientist, part aesthete, which characterizes so many birdwatchers today is a recent phenomenon.

More people than ever before care about birds today and more of them join bird societies in order to share their interest.

Birdwatching, whether as a science or a casual interest, is a poor thing if it consists mainly of a mad scramble to see the greatest number of species in the shortest possible time, though as a sport this is a perfectly valid occupation. It should never become a mere 'tally ho!' in pursuit of rarities. For most of us, birdwatching starts as an urge to put a name to birds seen. Goodness knows, that is difficult enough! But it develops into a desire to find answers to endless questions: 'Where have they come from?' 'Why are they here?' 'Where are they going?' The answers may be easy to find; sometimes they are near impossible. This book does answer some of the questions and it represents a simple introduction to bird history, biology and behaviour. It is for people who have begun to put a name to some of the birds on the bird table and who enjoy birds on the radio and television but want to move one stage further. I warn you that it provides little more than a taste of what birdwatching is about and that you will end up asking more questions, joining the bird societies and in real danger of becoming an ornithologist. You will never be bored again, for wherever you go in the world there will be birds, bird pleasures to enjoy and bird problems to solve.

Left: The changing fortunes of birds. A century ago herons were shot on sight in order to prevent valuable fishing rights. Nowadays most people (apart from fish-farmers!) regard them as a valuable part of the country scene.

Above: Great black-backed gulls at a whaling base in Iceland. Gulls have increased their numbers explosively as a direct consequence of man's extravagant waste of food.

2
Birds as Animals

Clouds of waders over an estuary.

All life on Earth originated in the seas. Plants were the first living things to colonize the land and they provided the vital life-support system that enabled animals to follow them ashore. The change-over from breathing water to breathing air was a slow process. First came the crawling and creeping creatures, without backbones; then came the amphibious fish, which learnt to 'walk' from puddle to puddle, finding easy prey among the insect swarms.

These primitive amphibians remained dependent on the water for the care and development of their soft eggs. In their juvenile stages, they floated free amid the plankton, as do the juveniles of most shore creatures still. It was only the development of a leathery egg-shell, which protected the embryo in its personal pool of amniotic fluid, that enabled the evolving reptiles to become independent of the sea and made them less vulnerable to predation in their early stages. Released from the necessity of entrusting their sexual products to the open waters, reptiles quickly dominated the land. They evolved in many directions, in many experimental forms. Their descendants included the dinosaurs and they established a variety of land-based techniques for living which stood the test of time and paved the way for the highly successful Classes of mammals and birds.

Archaeopteryx, the 'ancient winged one', was the link between true reptile and true bird. Fossil remains discovered in a Bavarian slate quarry in 1861 revealed the skeleton of a reptile, complete with toothed jaws and jointed tail but also displaying the distinct impressions of wing and tail feathers. This early cuckoo-like 'bird' lacked a keel to its breastbone, so its powers of flight may have been limited, but with the claws at the end of its arms it was probably able to clamber about in trees, gliding from one to another.

Archaeopteryx was not the only reptilian experiment in flying. Pterosaurs derived from quite different reptilian stock but also developed the hollow bones characteristic of birds. They flew on bat-like leathery wings extended between arms and feet. Like the dinosaurs, the pterosaurs achieved considerable success for a while but did not survive. Their bat-like skin flaps proved inconvenient for take-off and limited their range of abilities. They failed to develop feathers, the singular feature that enabled the descendants of *Archaeopteryx* to make such hugely successful experiments and to generate the Class of animals which persists today. Thanks to the use of

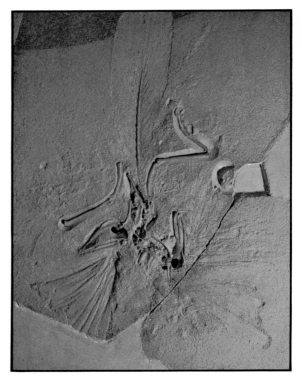

The first complete skeleton of *Archaeopteryx* was discovered in 1861, proving the existence of an intermediate form between reptiles and birds. The feathers are clearly to be seen. The animal probably flew much better than has been assumed in the past.

feathers, the arms alone were able to take care of flight, while legs and feet were freed to act as shock absorbers on landing and for all manner of adaptations, from walking and hopping to climbing, swimming and feeding.

Evidence of the reptilian ancestry of birds is apparent in certain shared characteristics between reptiles and birds; for example, in their eggs and in the general layout of the skeleton and musculature. The embryonic chick develops an egg-tooth as hatching time approaches, just as the reptile does. But only birds have feathers; no other Class of animal has this feature.

Despite its feathers, *Archaeopteryx* remained half-reptile, half-bird. The first true birds were creatures like *Ichthyornis* and *Hesperornis*, direct descendants of *Archaeopteryx*. They appeared some seventy million years later. Both of these birds still had reptilian teeth but nevertheless had developed a high degree of specialization. *Hesperornis* was a huge bird, more than six feet long, which fished by diving; its legs were set well back on the body in the manner of a present-day cormorant. *Ichthyornis* was also a seabird but smaller, more after the manner of a tern. It had a well-developed keel on the breastbone, suggesting that it had the sort of muscles needed by an accomplished flyer.

The two Orders these birds represent became extinct but other bird experiments produced more durable results. The golden age of experiment began during the Eocene period, 60 million years ago, when birds started to occupy every available ecological niche in an abundance of shape and life-style. The climate was balmy, warm and humid; the emerging birds hunted the insect-rich land and the fish-laden coral seas.

In the long process of testing, trial and error, research and development, only the fittest survived, according to the principles deduced by Darwin. Plants and animals produce more seed than is needed to maintain their numbers but only a proportion of young survive to breed and those which inherit characteristics favourable to survival are more likely to achieve that desirable goal. Those characteristics will be passed on to future offspring, so that favourable traits are perpetuated and unfavourable ones fail.

The Ice Ages presented a supreme test of bird fitness. The cycles of glaciation altered the landscape in brutal fashion: coral seas gave way to less enticing scenes. The resulting changes in climate and habitat, especially in high latitudes, put heavy pressure on all forms of life. Some 3,000 species of birds were unable to cope and became extinct. They lacked the essential capacity to adapt and change.

The survivors of any disaster are inevitably better equipped to face a repeat performance. We may safely assume that the birds which weathered the Ice Ages had learnt a great deal from their experience. Suitable migration patterns would have been heavily reinforced. This evolutionary process is continuous; it is known to scientists as adaptive radiation. In the course of time, the generations adapt to new environments or new life-styles and in the process they alter in form and structure to take best advantage of possibilities as they present themselves. For example, finches, which began as similar birds with similar tastes, slowly diverged as they became isolated on individual islands within a group which became separated from the mainland. The isolated communities branched out in different ways and eventually established separate specific identities.

Such changes may take many tens of thousands of years, or may occur explosively.

Conversely, creatures which represent entirely separate lines of ancestry may, by virtue of the fact that they live in the same countryside and hunt similar prey, come to look superficially alike. Owls and hawks have separate evolutionary backgrounds, yet both have hooked beaks and curved talons because they ply the same trade, albeit at different times of the day. This process is known as convergent radiation and it produces remarkable similarities of outward shape in species which are but distantly related. Divers and grebes provide another example of these look-alikes. With their long necks and pointed beaks, their paddle feet set well back on their bulky bodies, the divers are the nearest thing we can see today to those long-extinct birds like *Hesperornis*. They only lack teeth to look the part. Grebes, which are not closely related to divers, nevertheless dive and fish, seizing their prey in an underwater chase. Since the way of life of these two birds is similar, they have grown to share many characteristics.

Most of the bird models we see around us today are the direct result of the great Ice Age experience. They emerged a mere twenty million or so years ago, yet their ancestral roots stretch much further back. Not surprisingly, since we all came from the sea, waterfowl have the longest pedigrees and represent the more primitive bird characteristics. They date back some 115 million years. But the birds did not stop at the water's edge; they set out and colonized the whole of planet Earth. Four-fifths of our living species are now land-based, the product of recent geological time. The perching birds represent an Order of thrusting and successful newcomers, dating from only some sixty million years ago. While they may and often do derive advantage from being near fresh water, only rare examples such as the dipper actually feed in water and, while a surprising number of species may forage on the seashore, the vast majority of the passerines are out-and-out landlubbers, living in every kind of country, from desert to high mountain, from inner city to industrial wasteland. On migration they may be forced to cross the seas but it is a safe bet that, given the choice, they would avoid this dangerous undertaking.

Through these millions of years, the construction of the bird has changed greatly. *Archaeopteryx* was only a temporary, albeit vital, link with the past. The airframe and life-support systems of birds have altered, with their environ-

The light and rigid airframe of a bird provides housing
for a muscle system which powers wings and legs.

ment, to reach a high pitch of performance. Most changes have been in connection with flight but birds have also become better fitted for moving on land.

The forelimbs of the ancestral reptile became modified for flight. The arm, in many ways similar to our own arms, has lost some of the digits at its extremity in the process. The rib cage and backbone have fused, becoming a rigid airframe. In order to achieve lightness, the goal of all aircraft designers, the bones have become hollow and air-filled; the larger ones have grown internal struts for added strength. A keel extends from the breastbone to provide low-slung attachment (and centre of gravity) for the two mighty pectoral muscles, which provide the power to operate the wings and sustain flight. The major and minor pectorals (the white meat breast muscles of a chicken, for example) represent more than half of the bird's muscular tissue and indeed one fifth of the weight of the entire bird. Both are richly supplied with blood. The major pectoral powers the down-stroke of the wing, by way of fibres to the humerus (the upper arm), and the minor pectoral powers the up-stroke, which needs less effort. The Avian feet still bear traces of their ancestry in the shape of scales and claws. Skulls

have become compact and light. Where the reptilian teeth have disappeared, they have been replaced by a highly versatile beak.

Some of these changes have been by-passed by some birds, for good reasons. Diving birds have solid bones still. Lightness and buoyancy are less important to them than the ability to remain submerged for long periods without using energy. Their plumage, too, has adapted differently from that of birds which value the facility of airborne activity more highly. It would be a distinct disadvantage for diving birds to carry air trapped between their feathers and their skin down below the surface, so their plumage is, paradoxically, less waterproof than that of other birds. Thus we see that they float low in the water, showing less freeboard than those species which fly more readily. Diving birds carry their legs set well back on their bodies, so that their webbed feet operate in the most efficient manner under water, much as a ship's screw bites into the water at the stern. On land, they are unbalanced and at a disadvantage, waddling clumsily and never straying far from the safety of the water.

Legs come in different lengths. Herons, which spend a good deal of time stalking in the shallow water of a marsh or an estuary tide, have long

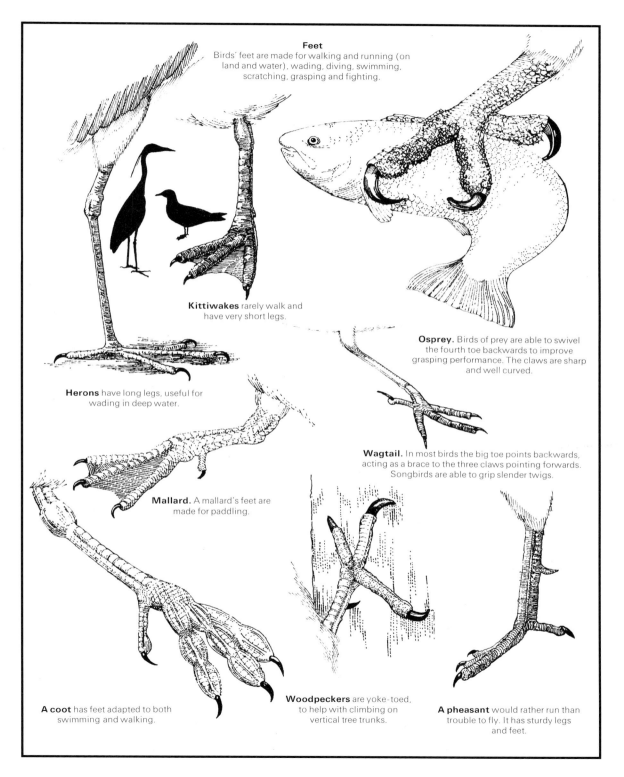

Feet
Birds' feet are made for walking and running (on land and water), wading, diving, swimming, scratching, grasping and fighting.

Kittiwakes rarely walk and have very short legs.

Osprey. Birds of prey are able to swivel the fourth toe backwards to improve grasping performance. The claws are sharp and well curved.

Herons have long legs, useful for wading in deep water.

Wagtail. In most birds the big toe points backwards, acting as a brace to the three claws pointing forwards. Songbirds are able to grip slender twigs.

Mallard. A mallard's feet are made for paddling.

A coot has feet adapted to both swimming and walking.

Woodpeckers are yoke-toed, to help with climbing on vertical tree trunks.

A pheasant would rather run than trouble to fly. It has sturdy legs and feet.

Short-eared owl *Asio flammeus*. This species hunts small mammals by daylight but like the other owls it has superb eyesight and hearing.

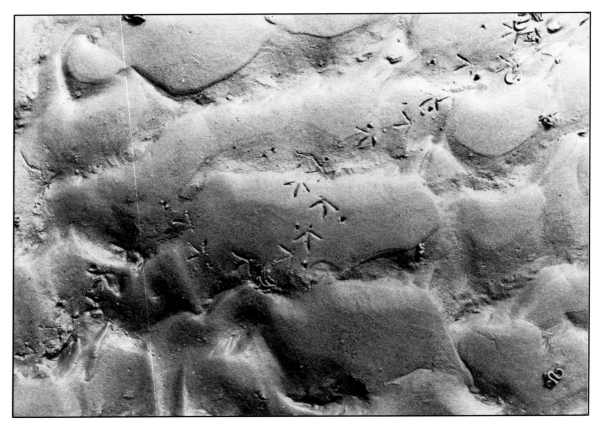

Bird footprints in sand. A wading bird, probably an oystercatcher, has passed this way. The tell-tale holes show where it has used its beak to probe for cockles or worms.

ones. Waders, which work closer inshore or over soft mud, have shorter ones. Swifts and kittiwakes, birds which only come to land with reluctance and do not walk at all, have hardly any legs worth talking about. Broadly speaking, the walkers and runners have long legs, the hoppers have short legs. Birds stand on their toes, their knees out of sight, hidden by the flank feathers of their plumage. When someone points to the zoo flamingo and remarks that its legs bend in the opposite manner to our own, they are simply mistaking the bird's heel, half-way between the ground and the feathers, for its knee.

In the same way that the terminal digits of the primitive forelimb have been reduced in the interests of the wing structure, the hind limb's five toes have been reduced to four. In most birds, the big toe points backwards, acting as a brace to the three claws that point forward, but in woodpeckers the toes are set in pairs, two in front, two behind (yoke-toed), to give a sure grip on the vertical trunks of dizzily tall trees. It has to be said that the bird also gets a lot of help in climbing from its stiff tail, which acts as a third leg, setting up a tripod effect.

Variations on foot shape allow birds to perch, run (on land and water), wade, swim, dive, scratch, grasp and fight. The perching songbirds of our gardens have that typical three-forward, one-astern layout, allowing them the facility of gripping slender twigs, grasses, reeds or clotheslines. They also have an invaluable device which allows them to go to sleep while perched on a twig, without dropping off when they relax. As their legs bend, when they settle into position, muscles tighten the flexor tendons which run down to the toes. These operate automatically, causing the toes to grip solidly, so that while the bird is crouched (but not when it stands up) it can relax without the fear of falling. This same facility brings advantage to birds of prey. When a sparrowhawk lands on a victim, its legs bend to

Bills

A bird's bill must do the work of teeth and it must
also serve as a hand. It is a
versatile tool.

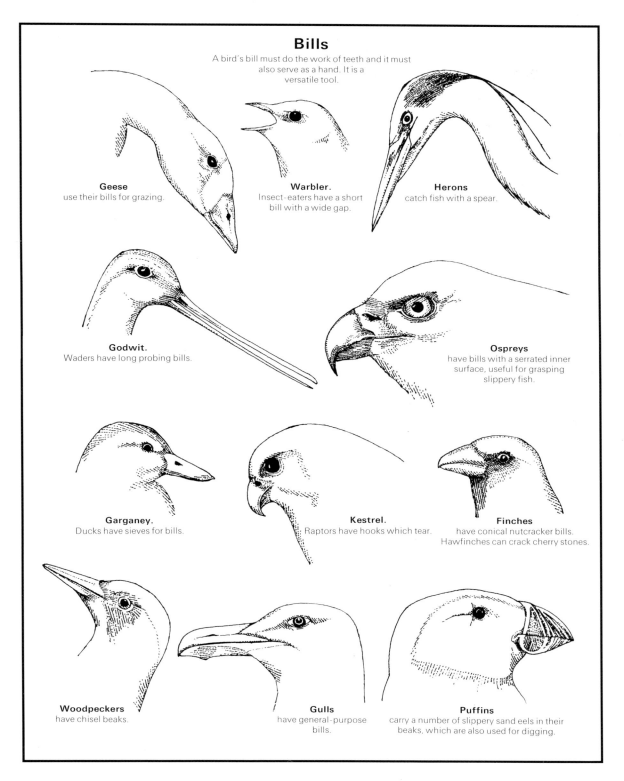

Geese
use their bills for grazing.

Warbler.
Insect-eaters have a short
bill with a wide gap.

Herons
catch fish with a spear.

Godwit.
Waders have long probing bills.

Ospreys
have bills with a serrated inner
surface, useful for grasping
slippery fish.

Garganey.
Ducks have sieves for bills.

Kestrel.
Raptors have hooks which tear.

Finches
have conical nutcracker bills.
Hawfinches can crack cherry stones.

Woodpeckers
have chisel beaks.

Gulls
have general-purpose
bills.

Puffins
carry a number of slippery sand eels in their
beaks, which are also used for digging.

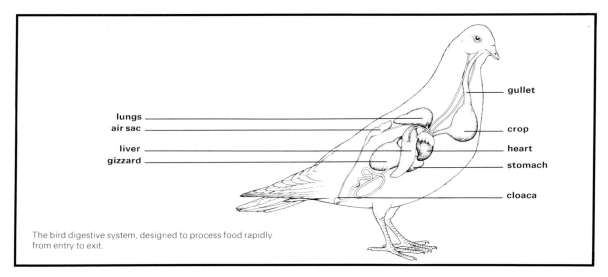

lungs
air sac
liver
gizzard

gullet
crop
heart
stomach
cloaca

The bird digestive system, designed to process food rapidly
from entry to exit.

absorb the impact. Automatically the talons grasp and imprison the unfortunate bundle of feathers, before it is carried off to be plucked and eaten. The process of eating brings another bird marvel into play; that is the bill, or beak (the words are interchangeable).

A bird's bill serves many purposes. It must do the job of teeth, which birds lack in the interests of lightness. It must also serve as a hand, since the bird's arms and hands have been devoted to the function of flight, and so it is used for picking up and manipulating food or building materials. It is a versatile tool: a hammer or a chisel, tweezers or nutcrackers; it can hook, spear, strain or tear. In both love and war it plays a part; in birth and parenthood it is vital, serving a multitude of needs. Without it, a bird could not even maintain its plumage.

The bill is a flexible projection of the jaws, sheathed in horn. It grows in much the same way as our finger-nails grow but the growth is compensated by normal wear and tear. At the very tip, there may be taste-organs and sensory nerve endings, which allow it to become a delicate instrument. On the other hand, it can be a blunt instrument, used to bludgeon and maim. Bills may be for general purpose or highly specialized. Finches have conical nutcracker bills which exert colossal pressure on nuts. Insect-eating birds tend to have short bills with a wide gape. Hooked bills deal with larger prey and in hawks they will be used to tear skin and meat. Waders have long probing bills for exploring soft mud, though oystercatchers carry a useful jemmy which can

deal with a cockle or mussel shell. Herons catch their prey with a fearsome spear. Mergansers, and ospreys for that matter, have bills whose inner surfaces are serrated in such a way that they can hold slippery fish. Ducks have sieves and geese have lawnmowers for bills. They come in all shapes and sizes and serve an astonishing variety of purposes. They may even act as advertising displays: the puffin sports an outer, highly coloured sheath, which peels off when its purpose of attracting a mate has been served and the breeding season is over.

Most birds lead active lives. They need large quantities of food to produce their energy and their digestive systems are designed to cope with a formidable throughput. First comes the crop, which is large and expansile in the case of seed and vegetable feeders, smaller for meat-eaters and virtually non-existent for owls, which bolt their mice whole. Then comes the stomach, which is in two parts. In the first part, the descending food is treated with digestive enzymes. The second part, the gizzard, is also lined with enzyme-producing tissue and is powered by strong muscular walls. Some birds may improve the milling function of the gizzard by swallowing small stones, which help to crush and prepare the hardest food. The abrasive stomach mill replaces the action of those reptilian teeth which were discarded millions of years ago. Seed-eaters have longer intestines than other birds, for the process of dealing with bulk food takes time. Carnivorous birds digest their meat rapidly. Berry-eaters, like the garden black-bird also process food quickly, voiding the pip as

Blackbird with its head cocked in typical 'listening' attitude. In fact it catches its worms by sight, its eye being roughly where we expect its ear to be!

little as a quarter of an hour after picking. This results in a seed encased in faecal material, all set to germinate in ideal conditions.

A bird's breathing arrangements are quite complicated. A pair of small lungs is linked to a complex network of air sacs which are distributed throughout the body, even in the hollow neck and trunk bones. These sacs act as storehouses for large amounts of air and may be associated with the bird's ability to alter its weight and to regulate its internal temperature. Buoyant sea ducks, like scoters, have the ability to sink down low in the water if they are alarmed, thus making themselves inconspicuous. The windpipe is an elastic tube, stiffened by rings of bone and cartilage. These rings allow the tube to bend freely but protect it from pinching or collapsing. When the bird's supple neck is twisted 'every which way' during preening, the outside air still has an open passage to the lungs.

At the point where the windpipe branches into two, serving the two lungs, there is a side-chamber called the syrinx, an organ of great significance to anyone who enjoys listening to bird song. Birds have a larynx but do not have vocal chords; instead, they have their unique syrinx. This varies in shape and complexity but consists of a resonating chamber equipped with membranes, operated by muscles along the outer walls. On exhalation, the air vibrates the membranes, producing sounds which vary from the quack of a mallard duck to the boxwood flute of a blackbird.

Birds have first class vision, in the superstar class. Their eyes are large, in proportion to their size, and are set in huge sockets. In fact, the eyes are much larger than they appear, for only the small cornea is visible; the greater part of the eyeball lies hidden in the skull. Birds' eyes have a semi-transparent extra lid, the nictitating membrane, which is drawn horizontally across the eye (except in the case of owls, when it operates vertically). Lubricated by tears, this membrane cleans the cornea. It may also provide underwater protection for diving birds.

Birds have an astonishing range of sight and different species see the world in totally different ways. For example, a blackbird's view of the world around him is quite unlike that of a sparrowhawk. Songbirds have eyes on the side of their heads, giving an all-round view, with the least perceptive vision dead-ahead. They have wide-angle lenses. Hunters, like hawks or gannets, have eyes set well forward on the head, giving the best possible forward vision. The effect is of binocular vision, with an overlapping field. This produces a 3-D effect, which allows for accurate range-finding. The buzzard can pinpoint a beetle even while he soars hundreds of feet in the sky. Buzzards have extra sharp sensitivity to movement, provided by a high density of cones in the central retinal area. This makes their sight something like three times more effective than our own. A herring gull can distinguish between a desirable crust of bread and an undesirable piece of orange peel from a great distance. Such abilities would be of little value to the blackbird, which works at ground level and short range. His all-round vision keeps a weather-eye for possible predators, while his lee-eye homes in on the early worm. Birds' eyes do not move about in their sockets, as ours do, so the blackbird must move his head to scan a different scene. In fact, he tends to hold his head still but steers a zigzag course across the lawn as he searches for food. When he catches a glimmer of movement at grass-level, he cocks his head in what looks to us exactly like a 'listening' attitude but his eye is where we instinctively feel his ear ought to be and, in fact, he is directing that eye to search the immediate area by his feet. Once he has a grip on the worm, his posture reverts to one which looks more natural to us and the tug-of-war begins.

Different birds have different sight patterns, by virtue of variations in the sensitivity of the light-cells in the retina; for example, owls have a highly developed response to weak light. Droplets of oil in the retinal cones act as colour filters, with exactly the effects achieved by photographers using coloured glass. Cameramen use yellow filters to emphasize white clouds in a blue sky on black and white film. Pigeons have a built-in yellow filter, which makes flying objects such as hawks stand out from their background. Kingfishers have their version of a polar filter (an excess of red droplets), which reduces glare and dazzle from water, a decided advantage to a fisherman.

Most owls are birds of the twilight and darkness and their visual acuity is accordingly well developed. Their skulls provide room for eyes which in some cases are bigger than those of a man. The eyes are set wide apart in a flat facial disc, which gives them superior forward vision. They have a narrow field of view but that field is covered to a large extent by both eyes so that their view is stereoscopic. In order to judge distance most accurately, they improve on the 3-D effect of the wide-set eyes by performing bobbing movements of the head, up-and-down and side-to-side. Try it yourself and see how much more precisely you can judge the range of an object. The owl needs information of this sort before committing himself to the fateful glide down to an unfortunate vole. Incidentally, owls cannot do the impossible: they cannot see in total darkness. There has to be a glimmer of light for them to use those magnificent eyes.

In conditions of poor light, owls are able to bring into play another of the more highly-developed bird senses, their acute hearing. It is tempting to think that the dished shape of an owl's face may even help to concentrate incoming sound waves in the manner of the sound recordist's parabolic reflector. Certainly, owls are able to hear the high frequency voices of the small rodents they are hunting. With their wide-set ears, they hear in stereo and are able to locate the direction of the sound source. If the mouse moves or squeaks, the hunting owl homes in to the attack.

A bird's hearing apparatus is broadly similar to our own. Although birds do not receive the lower end of the sound spectrum as well as we do, they have an extended reception at the upper range. Songbirds operate over a frequency range which extends from some 50 Hz to 20 kHz. It may be that, with rather closer-set ears than those of the larger predators, their extra high-pitch, urgent alarm calls are using a frequency which is uncomfortable for their enemies.

Unlike our own ears, those of most birds are recessed, so that they do not interrupt the aerodynamic flow of air during flight. For the same purpose, the ear-openings are covered by feathers but, at rest, these may be drawn aside to expose the reception dish when acute listening is called for. As in our ears, there is an otolith, or ear-stone, which plays an important part in the control of balance. Far back in our marine ancestry, this balance mechanism was doubtless the most important of the ear's functions; indeed, it still is for the fish. And it is still of vital importance for the flying birds, for the sensory hairs associated with the otolith convey information about attitude to the brain. On occasion, when coming ashore after prolonged exposure to the rolling and pitching of a small boat, for example, we ourselves may be reminded of the function of the otoliths; while they are temporarily 'unhinged', our bodies roll and pitch as we try to regain some sense of balance.

Birds are sensitive to touch but it is difficult to know how important this sense is to them. They have sensory nerve-endings under their skins and these presumably pass information to the brain about temperature and any painful phenomena with which they may come into contact. They also have sensors in feet and bills. Songbirds are aware of earth vibrations and waders are able to 'feel' the ground in a manner which will be examined in the chapter on food and feeding. They have no teeth with which to masticate and very few taste buds with which to enjoy food in the mouth. Presum-

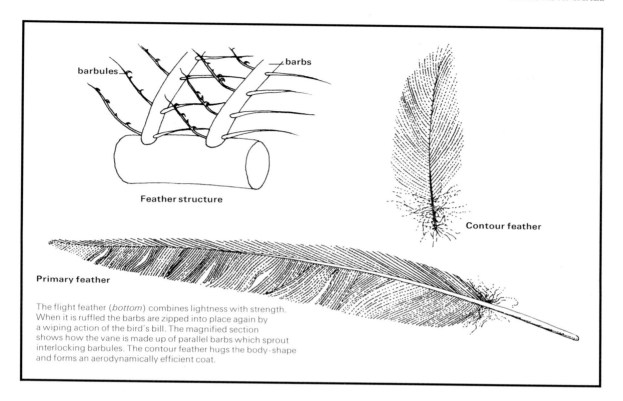

barbules

barbs

Feather structure

Contour feather

Primary feather

The flight feather (*bottom*) combines lightness with strength. When it is ruffled the barbs are zipped into place again by a wiping action of the bird's bill. The magnified section shows how the vane is made up of parallel barbs which sprout interlocking barbules. The contour feather hugs the body-shape and forms an aerodynamically efficient coat.

ably, their pleasure in feeding derives from the crop, which is well supplied with salivary glands.

The sense of smell is well provided for in the nervous system but in many cases is not greatly used, certainly by comparison with the mammals, which sniff out airborne chemicals with such ease. The only bird which relies heavily on smell for hunting is the kiwi, which works in the darkness, sniffing out earthworms. The job is done by nostrils at the tip of a long, probing bill. The flightless birds do have a better sense of smell than most other birds but it is probable that some seabirds, such as petrels and skuas, are able to locate floating offal by their sense of smell. In general, birds test potential food while in their bills by the limited use of taste and smell.

The nervous system is typical of other vertebrates and, not surprisingly, it matches that of the reptiles. There is one major difference, which is in the considerably larger size of the brain. It is slanderous to suggest that anyone who is a trifle on the slow side is a 'bird brain'. It used to be fashionable to suggest that birds do everything by blind 'instinct' and that they are computer-programmed, like robots, to behave in a particular

way in every event. Certainly, a great deal of a bird's behaviour is innate, in the sense that it is triggered by hereditary mechanisms. The cycle of breeding, for example, is heavily dependent on a well-established sequence of hormonal cues. But birds are perfectly capable of acting as individuals, displaying individual quirks and characteristics, and, on occasion, learning to their advantage. Their first marriage and their first breeding season may be a disaster but, if they survive, they go on to better things. They become used to noises and movements which prove harmless; they take evasive action in the face of recurring events which prove dangerous. Though, in many situations, they behave to a strict pattern with little variation, there are other situations in which they modify their actions to advantage. After the first blue tit discovered the truth about milk bottles, the news spread all over Britain like wildfire. That, after all, is what survival and natural selection are all about. In the same way, essential knowledge of flying is born with the chick but the knowledge is very basic. The first solo flight may be a pathetic attempt but a few circuits and bumps soon improve the performance.

Sociable in all activities except breeding, starlings typically bathe in parties. The object of the exercise is to wet the plumage without soaking the body, in preparation for preening.

The power of flight and flying performance is what marks birds apart from other creatures. In other Classes, only bats have developed the ability to any greater extent than the simple gliding of some fish, reptiles and squirrels and none of these have the benefit of the bird's secret weapon, the feather. A modified reptile scale, the feather has proved more versatile than the stretched skin of bats or the rigid skins of man-made aircraft. Add to this the bird's ability to repair or renew the feathers as they become damaged or worn out and the innovation seems almost miraculous. Certainly, it has been the object of much envy and men have spent an inordinate amount of time and energy in trying to enjoy the freedoms of the skies which it bestows.

Feathers are made of keratin, a protein secreted by skin cells, and they grow from skin follicles. Unlike human hair, they do not grow continuously but simply achieve their designed size. On the other hand, new growth will be stimulated if, for some reason, the feather is lost or, of course, at the onset of moult. The typical flight feather has a long, hollow quill, strutted and strengthened internally, reaching out to a solid tip. The working surface, the vane, is made up of a series of parallel barbs with interlocking barbules attached. The whole thing operates like a zip-fastener, so that if it is ruffled, or unzipped, the bird can run its beak along the feather and zip it up again. The structure is immensely strong, yet light and flexible.

Feathers serve several different purposes: the most obvious is flight but another important one is the creation of an outer coating that is aerodynamically sound. For this, the basic feather is shaped to suit the contours of the flying framework, smoothing the corners and hugging the body; at the inward end, there are downy filoplumes which provide extra insulation in addition to the specialized down feathers. Other feathers may serve as sensory organs or display signals during courtship or battle. Some even play a part as toilet preparations but, along with flight, the most important of a feather's functions is to provide weather-proofing and warmth. For this, they are well-greased on the outside and, to protect the inside, they overlap and trap a cushioned layer of air against the skin on the string-vest principle. A full suit will consist of several thousand feathers on a small bird, more than 25,000 on a swan.

Since feathers are obviously of vital importance to every facet of a bird's life, a great deal of care is devoted to their maintenance. In the normal course of events, feathers get dirty or become fouled with vegetation or food remains and there is always the possibility of unwelcome parasites, so the daily toilet takes up a great deal of a bird's time. Birds must bathe even in the depths of winter. Unless the plumage is healthy and in good working order, a bird has little protection from the cold and an impaired ability to fly from trouble or to food. Even though the act of bathing exposes the animal to danger, it must indulge. When you provide a birdbath, an essential for any bird garden, make sure that there is dead ground all round it, to give the birds a chance to see the cat before it arrives. There is no need for deep water; a shallow dish offering a choice of depths down to four inches (10 cm) at the most is ideal. The shallow end of a weedy pond serves very well.

The object of the bath is to wet the plumage without actually soaking it. (You will notice that although birds may actively bathe in drizzle, they dislike a downpour and hunch themselves in such a way that the water runs off quickly.) Squatting in the water, the bird ruffles its body and tail feathers open and creates a shower of spray by beating and whirling its wings. With the plumage erected, the splashing drops can get between the feathers and the skin. As the skin is well protected by a greasy surface, there is no danger of saturation. Then the head is dunked underwater and the head and breast are pushed from side to side as the beak flicks more water about. Finally, the foreparts lift in a see-saw as the tail is spread and splashed to get its share of washing. Water birds bathe for exactly the same reasons as land birds. Both fresh- and salt-water species duck and splash. If they have a chance, seabirds will always prefer bathing in fresh water.

Sparrows bathe in dust as well as water. Dipping in the garden pond one day, they may choose a dry spot in the flower border the next. There is even an extraordinary tale of a gang of sparrows which used the sugar bowl in a works canteen for bathing. They settled into the sugar bath just as if it were a dust bowl, wriggling and wing-flicking and throwing the dry sugar all over

Birds do not only bathe in water. House sparrows bathe in dust.

Blackbirds bathe themselves in ants. All these activities are related to the chore of feather maintenance.

the table. As well as the domestic chicken, gamebirds like partridges bathe in dust, kicking it on to their backs and through the plumage, an indication of their arid ancestry.

Most surprising of all techniques is the widespread practice of bathing in ants. Blackbirds or jays, for example, may perform this activity on the lawn or terrace when there are suitable ants in abundance. They prefer the species which defend themselves by squirting formic acid or other pungent fluids. The birds pick them up deliberately and place them on their feathers, especially on the wing tips, or they may simply squat down and spread their plumage in such a way that the ants swarm all over their bodies.

Sunbathing also has practical value to the birds and, given the opportunity, they will readily

27

Many birds enjoy sunbathing. This blackbird is in the typically abandoned position, displaying its wing and tail feathers to the sun and absorbing ultra-violet light.

indulge. Garden birds typically crouch down, fluff their feathers and droop their wings, showing their backs to the sun, or they may lie flat on the ground with both wings and tail stretched out. Owls prefer the style of Scandinavian beauties, turning their faces to the hot sun. Pigeons, on a sheltered rooftop, lie right over on one side with the opposite wing stretched out and raised, so that the sun warms their flanks. They seem to enjoy the process and it probably does them good. One possible value is that the ultraviolet light of the sun acts on the preen oil on their feathers, producing vitamin D which they ingest during the next round of preening. The sun may also wake up the parasites on the bird's body, giving the host a chance to catch them.

Whether the birds are bathing in water, sun, rain, smoke, dust or ants, the component movements of the activity are much the same and the next phase of the toilet, preening, is equally stereotyped. This is a process which may take anything from a few minutes to more than an hour. The bird retires to a safe place, shakes off excess droplets from its bath and dries itself. Ruffling the plumage, it shakes and rattles the wing and tail tips to rid itself of moisture. Next, it

Wings

Birds' wings are highly sophisticated pieces of equipment. Different shapes serve different purposes.

Low aspect-ratio: pigeons have the facility of vertical take-off and fast flapping.

High aspect-ratio: the long, narrow wings of a gannet make for superb endurance but poor close-quarters manoeuvring.

Gulls have general-purpose wings, of medium aspect-ratio, giving good all-round flying characteristics.

The swift's sickle-shaped wing gives it mastery of the sky as a high-speed acrobat.

Peregrines are the fastest of all birds.

Razorbill.
Auks have the best of both worlds. Their short, narrow wings give fast buzzing flight in air, while a slower flapping rate propels them through the dense medium of seawater.

Hawks are fairly fast, but their broad wings allow them to manoeuvre round tree trunks and hedgerows in the chase.

Kestrels are able to hover with dexterity, a facility which uses a great deal of energy.

A pheasant has broad, short wings. It can escape trouble with a rocket-like departure, but has low flying endurance.

Cock bullfinch preening. Having dressed the plumage with oil, he treats each flight feather with individual attention, zipping it into trim with his beak.

cleans its bill by wiping it or stropping it against a perch and then proceeds to extract preen oil from the prominent gland above the root of the tail. This gland secretes a waxy substance which, smeared on the outer coat of feathers, acts as a water-repellent. Not surprisingly, it is particularly efficient in water birds, or birds which make a habit of diving into water, like the osprey.

The flight feathers are dressed with the oil and carefully zipped into airworthiness in case of emergency. Then, at leisure, the oil is worked into the plumage systematically, transferred from the oil gland by the bill to each feather in turn, as a dressing and waterproofing. The scratching and rubbing movements involved in this activity are infectious. In a flock, if one bird starts preening, they will all quickly follow suit, rather like a roomful of people yawning. The movements have a large element of comfortable ritual about them. The bird cannot reach its head feathers with its oily beak, so it uses its feet, first to comb and then to transfer oil from the bill to the head. Birds with long enough necks may be able to oil their heads directly by reaching them back to the oil gland. Some species of birds which have a tendency to sit

shoulder-to-shoulder or nest in close company preen each other. This social preening may involve an element of reward, since the head area is well populated with lice. These lice, incidentally, live on the feathers themselves, clinging fast and eating the barbules.

Some birds, like the bittern and heron, have a flattened, serrated claw, a toothcomb, on their third toes. They tend to spend more time at preening than other birds because they have particular problems. Herons specialize in eating eels, which are not only slimy but wriggly and reluctant to give in; the act of catching, mastering and swallowing them leaves the captor's contour feathers in a filthy mess. With head and neck covered in eel-slime, the heron solves the problem of preening with the aid of the toothcomb claw and a powder puff. The powder comes from patches at the base of the neck and just under the wings, where specialized feathers have a tendency to disintegrate and are so friable that when they are rubbed with the bill they crumble into dust. The bird buries its head under the wing, shakes or strokes the bill gently, or sometimes not so gently, first one side and then the other, till its head is quite covered by powder. It transfers the powder down by means of its bill to the remaining slimy feathers, using the toothcomb on its foot to comb away the powder, complete with slime. By this time the plumage is in disarray and somewhat dry. So the bird must proceed to normal preening and oiling by way of the preen gland under its tail coverts. One way and another, the job will probably have taken an hour.

Feathers are well used and they suffer a good deal of wear and tear. Individual feathers which suffer injury or accident are re-grown and replaced

Wrestling with eels leaves a heron's head and neck covered with slime. He has a specially designed toothcomb on one of his toes to help with preening.

as necessary but the entire plumage of a bird is replaced on a regular basis, so that periods of moult are part of the annual cycle. The process varies for different species, according to their life-style. Most of our garden birds moult two or three times in the year but they shed flight and tail feathers in a balanced fashion, matching a left for a right, so that, although they may be operating at reduced efficiency for a while, they do have a fair degree of warmth, waterproofing and flight capability all the time.

Many water birds moult their flight feathers in one fell swoop, enduring a period of flightlessness, when they are very vulnerable to predators. At this time, when males are said to be in eclipse plumage, they tend to congregate in large numbers in remote places where there is ample food and a distinct lack of disturbance. For some weeks, they are restricted to swimming or walking.

When the uncomfortable period of moult is over, the bird parades a new suit and is again in full flying order. The capability of feathered flight is the solution to many problems and the key to world travel. A tern may spend our summer nesting in the Arctic, then strike south to 'winter' in the Antarctic summer. That may seem incredible to us but, from the bird's point of view, it is simply making the best of both worlds. Not all flight is on a global scale. Many feats are possible with feathers: instant escape from enemies, airborne invasion of an area newly rich in caterpillars, or fast approach and capture of prey.

Even for flightless birds, which might at first seem to make nonsense of all those years of research and development, the wings are important pieces of equipment. A penguin's flipper may seem an unfeathered, hard and rigid structure but it is in fact a modified wing superbly built for flying underwater. The bird is a master submariner.

The wings of a bird are highly sophisticated pieces of equipment. The primary flight feathers are joined to the bones of the bird's 'hand', which has a reduced number of fingers. Secondary feathers are joined to the forearm and their function is to provide lift, while the primaries provide propulsion and control surfaces in conjunction with the tail. The wing is thicker and blunter along the leading edge, tapering to a thinner, trailing edge; it is convex on top, concave underneath, favouring lift and offering a smooth passage to the flow of air. The whole assembly is flexible and powerful, the power being provided by the low-slung muscles on either side of the keel.

Marsh harrier making a controlled slow-speed landing at its nest, carrying food for the chick in its left foot. Note the 'bastard wing' spread out ahead of the primaries.

In the terms of a man-made aircraft, the bird's wings are acting both as wings and engine, giving lift and thrust, but man's version is crude, for his greater speed and height is gained only at the expense of vastly greater use of fuel. Many of the sophisticated techniques used to achieve slow-speed manoeuvrability in aircraft are paralleled by birds. Most obviously, the slots which delay stalling on a plane are catered for in birds by the so-called 'bastard wing', which consists of small quills attached to the thumb. Watch pigeons coming in to land on a crowded city square and you will soon see what remarkable slow-speed control these slot feathers allow, as the birds jockey for possession of a minimal landing space.

Aspect ratio, the relationship between wing length and average width, is an indicator of a bird's life-style. Soaring and gliding are activities best achieved with long narrow wings. Fulmars are good examples of this high aspect ratio. As ocean

travellers, they spend a lot of time in the air and have great endurance but are at a disadvantage in landing and take-off or any close-quarters manoeuvre which calls for rapid acceleration. Vertical take-off and fast flapping is the prerogative of birds with low aspect ratios. Pigeons provide a good example, with their relatively short, broad wings. Pheasants also have broad, short wings, powered by plenty of muscle, giving them the vital ability to take off like a rocket, accelerating away from trouble only to land, out of breath and out of sight, just round the corner, where they will need to rest and refuel.

The most aerial of all birds is the swift, whose sickle-shaped wing is the epitome of high aspect ratio, giving it the seemingly effortless mastery of the sky. On the rare occasions when it has to land, it manages to do so only with a clumsiness which is almost painful to watch, though its claws are sharp as needles, allowing it to cling to vertical walls and

Long narrow wings give a fulmar mastery of soaring and gliding. They have long-distance endurance at sea, but are at a disadvantage in manoeuvres which call for evasive action or fast acceleration. Nowadays they are a common sight off British clifftops.

rock faces. In order to reduce its all-up payload, the feet are tiny, just adequate to enable the bird to stagger to its nest. By the same token, the seagoing kittiwake has short legs, albeit provided with powerful paddles, since it does not expect ever to go for a walk.

Falcons are typically speedy fliers. The peregrine, reputedly the fastest of all birds, reaches the best part of eighty miles an hour in a power dive. But the hawks, although not lacking speed, tend to have broader wings. The sparrowhawk, operating along hedgerows and spinneys, has relatively short, rounded wings which give it a high degree of round-the-tree-trunk manoeuvrability when engaged in the chase. Kestrels and terns have

Whitethroat. A typical hedgerow and nettle-patch bird. Its general-purpose wings allow it to manoeuvre at close quarters and to disappear quickly into the depths of a bramble bush when a sparrowhawk appears.

the uncommon facility of hovering, seemingly motionless, in the air, a feat which taxes the wings and is energy intensive but clearly pays off in terms of hunting success.

Gulls are examples of the many species which have general purpose wings, a medium aspect ratio, so that they have good all-round flying characteristics, medium endurance and more than adequate take-off and landing performance. Auks have something of the best of two different worlds. Their short, narrow wings give them fast buzzing flight when they are flapped hard; their paddle feet serve as air-brakes on landing, then as rudders underwater, when the wings reduce the flap rate and propel the bird through the much denser medium. Even on land, the auks manage to waddle about with reasonable facility, though they need to stretch out their wings to keep themselves balanced. One way and another, they seem admirably adapted to diverse life-styles and it is no surprise that they are one of the most numerous of families, despite their present-day difficulties with oil-slicks.

When large numbers of birds are in the air together, it may seem astonishing to us that they never appear to collide but doubtless to them their air traffic control system is more than adequate. A cloud of waders on an estuary regularly changes direction in a manner that looks suicidal to a grounded birdwatcher. The birds drill with the precision of a brigade of guards, turning and swooping apparently simultaneously, but in fact it is a case of the quickness of the hand deceiving the eye. They do not turn and manoeuvre like a brigade of guards. One bird changes course, his

33

near neighbours follow suit, then their neighbours do likewise and so on. In due course, the whole flock has changed direction. This all happens in such a short time that the human eye is hardly able to keep up with it but, if you slow down the action by exposing high-speed movie film, frame by frame analysis proves that the manoeuvre is not simultaneous but sequential.

Soaring and gliding birds take advantage of the free lift provided by up-currents of air. Physical features like cliffs, slopes, hills and even waves encourage air masses to rise and the well-equipped bird profits from this. At sea, the albatrosses and petrels are the masters; on land, the hawks and vultures take over. Soaring conditions improve as the sun gets higher in the sky, so soaring birds, unlike most others, are late risers. Not for them the dawn patrol that catches the early worm as it enjoys the damp grass. First thing in the morning, a vulture must flap if he wants to fly and he is likely to be working at low altitude. As the atmosphere warms up, the thermal up-draughts allow the bird to adjust its whole wing surface for lift and it circles in easy loops, gaining height and a commanding view of its hunting territory. Slotted primary feathers provide extra lift.

High flying would be a waste of effort for nocturnal owls. Working the night shift, they do not even have the option of a thermal up-draught. But owls have their own highly-developed techniques for successful flying. In many ways, owls are deceptive creatures. They look plump and cuddly, yet the generous plumage conceals a vicious set of claws and a surprisingly skinny bird. The broad, generous wings support the lightly loaded airframe with great ease. With no need for panicky flapping, the owl glides about its business with buoyancy and a high degree of control. It has sacrificed high speed but gained important rewards. Its most impressive and disconcerting trick is to fly in silence, whispering along the side of the road or past the gravestones in the churchyard, its own listening apparatus unhampered by noisy flapping. To help achieve this ghostly effect, the owl has a specially developed feather structure. The long primary pinions are finely fringed at the edges and have a velvety pile on the surface. Being aerodynamically less efficient, this involves greater use of energy but spare power is readily available. The sacrifice of speed pays off. The voles and field mice do not see or hear the slow approach of nemesis until it is too late.

We have seen that birds come in all shapes and sizes, of a complexity of character and life-style that at first sight beggars description, yet, if we are to come to any kind of understanding of an uncountable number of individuals, we have to group them together and pigeon-hole them in some way. We need to put a name to the thing in which we are interested. People have been putting names to birds ever since men were able to speak but the problem of naming and sorting them in a manner acceptable to scientific study has proved altogether more complex.

Some birds, especially those which have distinctive physical features, have acquired a whole quiver of local names. Thus the puffin is known as a bottlenose in Wales, a parrot-billed willy in Sussex, a sea-parrot in Norfolk, a tammie norie in Shetland, a pipe or a pope in Cornwall. It is also known as a Londoner in the far west of Cornwall, possibly because of its tendency to stand about on a cliff slope, staring vacantly out to sea, or perhaps because of the evening wear favoured by pre-war visitors to the posher hotels! If some order and understanding is desired, then there has to be a common name which brings instant recognition to ornithologists at least. This is the justification for the scientific naming system. While a little brown bird in the garden may be a hedge sparrow to some and a dunnock to others, it is *Prunella modularis* all the world over. The value of scientific names is that, being based on a dead language, Latin, they are not subject to the sort of changes brought about by time and common usage, which give words different meanings in different decades. The value of an ossified language is beyond price to the taxonomist who catalogues living creatures.

The problems of classification are immense and, at first sight, seemingly insoluble. Groupings by size or colour or habitat, which might seem practical, become impossible as soon as you get to the drawing board. Too many birds are much the same size; the colour variations are too complex and vary through the life of the bird and its annual cycle; birds may breed in one kind of country, disperse to another and winter in yet another, so a habitat classification is not the answer. The accepted system is to place the bird in the context of its evolutionary history. Putting aside superficial similarities or differences, the systematist concentrates on the character of the bird's skeleton and musculature, the structure of its feet and mouth. He looks for anatomical clues to its ancestral background. This sort of genealogical work separates the owls from the hawks and the grebes from the divers and provides us with a firm framework which categorizes birds in a sequence working from the 'primitive' (those with the oldest established roots in time) to the 'advanced' (those most recently developed, the passerines), with crows or sparrows representing the peak of evolutionary excellence and complexity. These large-brained birds spearhead evolution. Opportunists and unspecialized jacks-of-all-trades, they are well-suited to take advantage of whatever world they must come to terms with: an admirable trait for modern times.

Scientists and philosophers struggled for centuries to devise a practical filing system. It was in 1735 that the Swedish naturalist Linnaeus published his watershed work *Systema Naturae*, which established the biological principles for listing plants and animals. One of the great joys of the system is that it re-affirms our common ancestry with all other life forms. Not only are we alive and they alive but we are directly related, just as truly as we are linked with our own parents, grandparents, cousins, aunts, friends and enemies alike. We may feel and look different from the robin in the garden but we come from the same root source.

Linnaeus's principle was to list into ever smaller groupings those plants or animals which displayed similarities with each other. His object was to give a name and provenance to every living thing. Working from the top, he proposed plant and animal Kingdoms. Then, he divided the animals (everything from an elephant to a sandhopper) into twenty-two (some would say twenty-three) branches (Phyla), one of which encompasses the vertebrates, the animals with backbones. This Phylum Chordata is further divided into a number of Classes, one of which is for mammals, where we ourselves are placed, and another for birds, the Class of Aves. There are twenty-six Orders of birds. These Orders are major groupings within the Class. For example, one Order is for the perching birds (or songbirds). These are the Passeriformes, which contain over a third of all living Families. The Family is the next sub-division. Within the Family, a group of closely related birds with common traits of behaviour or plumage or structure represent a Genus, which is finally divided into Species, the 'kinds' of bird which we all recognize as separate creatures, even those of us who say we do not know a twite from a linnet!

By definition, a Species consists of individuals which group together to form a viable breeding stock and whose offspring reproduce true; that is, they are reproductively isolated from other groups. A bird is known by its generic name suffixed by its specific name, so that a blue tit, *Parus caeruleus*, belongs to the tit Family (Paridae) which is part of the songbird Order of the bird Class of the vertebrate branch of the Animal Kingdom.

Before we draw breath, it is important to say that it is not as simple as I hope I have made it appear. There are further divisions of subphyla and sub and super families, tribe and so on. There are subspecies, whose members have some characteristics which differ from the established specific form. This may be a difference in plumage, perhaps, which has its origin in the distribution of the bird. Thus, American house sparrows have a subtly different plumage to our British house sparrows and they sport an extra name, tagged on to the conventional binomial description, to give them subspecific trinomial status. Subspecies are representatives of the 'grey' period, during which the process of evolution is developing a new species. During this period, the subspecies is still interbreeding with the parent stock, while working towards the truly specific status of reproductive isolation.

The Linnaean system, though devised at a time when the accepted assumption was that living creatures had been divided once and for all into convenient groups by a 'Master Plan', nevertheless served the subsequent Darwinian concept of evolution perfectly, in that it saw life forms in the framework of their relationships. Not surprisingly, there has been a continuing dialogue between scientists about the validity of Linnaeus's listings and there is endless scope for systematic nit-picking in the discussion of status and classification. Inevitably, opinions change and, with them, the Linnaean nomenclature. Nowadays, names are promulgated by an International Committee as the International Code of Zoological Nomenclature. Although the resulting lists have generated much disagreement and controversy, it has to be generally accepted that an agreed sequential listing of families, genera and species is vital for the purposes of filing, publishing and so on. Of the various lists which have been fashionable, the current version is that of a Dutch professor, K. H. Voous. Inevitably, taxonomic research will overturn the Voous List (see pp 198–204) in time but at least the pious aim is to promote stability.

3
Food
and
Feeding

Barnacle geese grazing winter pasture.

Many birds operate at a high metabolic rate. Small ones, especially, burn their food energy fast and lose a lot of heat through their proportionately large body surface. They need to work long hours to gather enough food to keep going. The wren has a giant's appetite in direct contrast to his size. The great diversity of species is able to flourish because of the way in which birds have learnt to exploit a variety of food sources, living cheek by jowl with neighbours who indulge different tastes. Several species live together in near-harmony because they have developed complementary adaptations and occupy slightly different ecological niches. Various members of the tit family may visit the same tree but they forage at different heights and for subtly different prey.

Each kind of country produces its own characteristic bird list: wide-ranging birds of prey hunt over endless sweeps of moorland; hawks and small birds work the woods and woodland edge; crows and plovers enjoy the farmer's company; long-legged waders haunt the mud and reedy marshes; seabirds fish the seas. Each habitat experiences a seasonal flow of visitors which come to harvest a particular crop. No habitat, however inhospitable it may seem to us, is without a bird of some sort to sample its delights.

All flesh is grass, of course, and one Order of birds goes straight to the fields. Many of the swans, geese and ducks feed almost exclusively on green plants; their bills have serrated edges for mowing the grass. One of the most exciting spectacles in birdwatching is to see flights of wildfowl rocketing down to the remote grassfields of the Solway Firth or the Hebrides. On the other hand, many a farmer takes a jaundiced view of the massed geese grazing their way across his winter wheat. But research has shown that, in most cases, the cropping does little if any damage. The growing plants are not at a stage when trampling harms them and the birds' nitrogen-rich droppings are a fair repayment for the shoots they take. Yields may even be significantly higher from fields visited by geese.

Brent geese, seasonal visitors fleeing the Siberian winter, are often in trouble with farmers. Part of the problem is that they have increasing difficulty in finding areas where they may graze in their traditional manner on the marine eel-grass, *Zostera*. This unpretentious plant grows on shallow sand-flats at the mouths of estuaries, just the sort of place where we like to build airports or yacht marinas.

Not all the wildfowl are specialist grazers. The ducks, especially, go in for a variety of feeding techniques. Widgeon are typical marsh grazers but other ducks hoover the soft surface mud, dabble or dive in both fresh and salt water or go in for full-scale fish-hunting at sea. The sea ducks, like scoters and mergansers, use their saw-toothed bills to grasp fish caught in an underwater chase. Their dabbling, duck-pond relatives have rows of horny ridges along the mandible edges, which serve as sieves to strain small particles of food from the muddy water.

Group activity is typical of the waterfowl and also of families like the gulls. Birds of a feather flock together, sometimes at least. There are decided advantages in this behaviour. When lots of birds are searching for food, one of them is likely to find it, so the rest can share in the success. Obviously, the food needs to be in abundance when they do find it. Hundreds of acres of grass will satisfy a regiment of geese but a bird hunting rabbits or mice is going to be better off working solo. Also, there has to be a degree of safety in the isolated working area. The geese are careful to graze at a good distance from likely trouble and to keep a good look-out. Other birds wear drab, camouflaged plumage and stay out of sight.

Many small birds go in for active hunting in company. Long-tailed tits will work their way through the hedgerow trees, keeping loosely in touch with a constant chirping. This way, they all benefit from the discovery of a choice food-site. Starlings are typically gregarious, at least outside the breeding season. They actually prefer to work together in noisy crowds. They will eat almost anything; they are quick to find food and quick to move on when it is exhausted, to search for fresh fields. Whatever they do, they do it together. When one feeds, they all feed; when one bathes, they all bathe. They are social birds, with a built-in tendency to flock, and one of the characteristics of a flock is this synchronization of activity. They all fly together, turn together, feed together, drink together, sing together.

There must be great advantage in subscribing to a social community of this kind. It gives stability. Law and organization are as valuable to a bird society as they are to the human version. Working together as a group, they feed more effectively, as we have seen. They can also survive attacks by predators, by sticking closely together and relying on safety in numbers. If a predator has to be tackled, it is easier done with combined forces.

Ducks indulge in a variety of feeding techniques: grazing, dabbling and diving. Pintails reaching down for plants on the bottom.

Starlings are even typically sociable with other species. They will fly in and forage on open fields with groups of lapwings, rooks and jackdaws. I have seen them working the strandline of a beach, busily snatching sandhoppers from rotting seaweed in company with turnstones. They will graze alongside a herd of cattle, taking the insects disturbed by the cows' feet as they swish through the grass, for all the world as if they were cattle egrets. They will do the same among a flock of sheep, with whom they have an even more intimate relationship, for they jump right up and find the ticks which parasitize the woolly backs. Perhaps not quite so welcome, they will follow green woodpeckers as they work a lawn for ants, picking up the strays.

Starlings are busy workers on the ground, covering the country with a purposeful walk, sometimes running, sometimes hopping. They feed in close flocks, the individuals evenly spaced, separating the grasses, probing the top layers of the soil, searching out leatherjackets and other larvae, the worms and insects, the teeming life of the soil. In spring they take a tithe of the cereal crops and in autumn they enjoy ripe fruit but, as far as man is concerned, their balance sheet probably works out on the 'good' side, as they are useful birds to the farmer. Like the titmice, they will take caterpillars in quantity.

In winter, starlings depend heavily on leatherjackets during the mild spells which favour them; in colder conditions, they look for grain and, to a lesser extent, beetles and snails. The bird is a supreme opportunist, taking advantage of whatever is most freely available at any given time. That is how it survives conditions which test other small birds beyond their limits.

Another opportunist is the robin, which has learnt to take advantage of bread-and-butter when it is offered, yet can manage perfectly well without the help of man. Originally a bird of woodland edge, it has taken with enthusiasm to the flowering of suburbia, where both the fruit-and-veg allotments and the bird tables provide it

Left above: Starlings at bird table.
Left below: Great and blue tits at a peanut dispenser.
Above: Great spotted woodpeckers are enthusiastic suet-eaters.

Bird tables and the various feeding devices offer an effective way of encouraging birds to show themselves where you see them to advantage, particularly in winter.

41

with a comfortable living. The robin tends to perch on a branch, keeping a sharp eye on the surroundings. When an insect shows itself, he makes a brief sortie to collect it and returns to the perch, rather in the manner which the spotted flycatcher has made its speciality. In the wild, the robin's food is mainly insects, especially beetles and flies, but it will take spiders and earthworms freely enough, with some fruit, berries and weed seeds. It is clear why they are such enthusiastic gardeners, always ready to join in with a spot of digging.

Robins are also keen bird-table customers, prepared to sample anything. Their bird-table technique is much the same as their typical twig-to-ground forays for wild food: appraisal from a safe distance, then the firm approach and grab, followed by removal of the food to a safe place for enjoyment. They will soon learn to come and tap on the window for a daily ration of currants or sultanas and, though it takes them a long time to grasp the technique, some individuals have learnt to exploit the bounty of a peanut-feeder.

There is no doubt that bird tables and feeding devices do a great deal to keep suburban bird populations high in the winter, when natural food is hard to come by. If you live in the southern part of Britain, you may well have a blackcap wintering in your garden, though the vast majority of its like have fled south, and it may well be that bird-table food keeps the individual going, though it will also be glad of your *Cotoneaster* and honeysuckle berries and any rotting apples left on the ground. Blackcaps will eat holly berries but not ivy, except as a last resort, and they have been seen with ripe mistletoe berries, which are usually the prerogative of the thrushes. In other words, the occasional blackcap survives our British winter because it can tolerate a variety of foods. In the case of the specialist insect eater, it is only the exceptional individual which can survive without migrating. There are records proving that some swallows have managed it but the number must be very small. Shortage of food compels the overwhelming majority to leave our shores in October, only to return in the insect-rich days of mid-April.

Swallows, along with house-martins and swifts, are birds of the open air, wheeling and skimming over new-mown pasture, around the grazing cattle, past the broad-leaved trees with their buzzing insect life, and hawking the hordes of flying ants when they take to thermal up-draughts on their wedding flights. These birds are specially designed to catch insects on the wing; flies, beetles,

Swallows are specially designed to catch insects on the wing.

moths and butterflies are all legitimate prey. They feed entirely on insects, mostly catching them in the air but also picking them off the surface of open water. The short, broad bills open to a wide gape as they fly, scooping the unfortunate prey as if with an aerial shrimp net. At the sides of the mouth are modified contour feathers, which bristle out as if they act to funnel the insects in to their doom, though there is no proof that this is the case. The system certainly works. Watch the aerial hunters on a fine calm day and listen to the constant clicking of their beaks as they fill up with a payload of gnats.

When you consider the indigenous populations of insect-eating birds, increased in the summer months by an invading horde of warblers and hirundines and swifts, it may seem astonishing that any insect can survive to breed but of course the over-riding rules of the chase decree that the very last event will be the extermination of the food-species which is the quarry of the hunter. No natural predator ever brings about the extermination of its prey; instead, the long-term effect is to produce a comfortable balance between the two. When insects flourish, their predators flourish, and when insects face hard times, so do their prey. There is a lot of sense, for a bird, in being able to look around for alternative supplies.

Blue tits, for example, actively seek out and destroy, or rather recycle, great quantities of caterpillars, bugs and larvae of all kinds. They are in their element in an orchard, earning the fruit grower's gratitude by taking large numbers of caterpillars of the codling moth, which damage many apples. They will also eat a variety of seeds, from wheat to beechmast and pine; given the chance, they will enjoy sunflower seeds and a mountain of peanuts. On balance, they are an asset to any garden, but they eat 'good' insects, which the gardener would prefer them to leave alone, just as freely as they eat 'bad' ones.

It is true that in springtime the tits will attack buds but they are not alone in that activity. On occasion they will lie in wait outside a beehive to pick off honey bees, which does not make them popular with beekeepers. In some parts of the country, tits were known as bee-birds because of this habit. On a cold day, when the insects will be torpid, they may actually enter the hive. Though most people may think of tomtits as the most charming and inoffensive of birds, you only need to watch one deal with a bee to think again. It holds the insect down firmly with a foot and hacks it open with its bill in the style of an eagle. In Devon, tomtits were once known as 'hackymals', a direct reference to this devastating technique. They are well able to deal with the bee's poison, rubbing the insect against a perch and discharging the venom before eating the meat. Both bumble bees and wasps are dealt with in like manner. However, the blue tits do not always have it their own way: there are records of wasps driving them away from ripening fruit and they have been seen to be wary of investigating a bone upon which wasps were already feeding.

Robins will also feed on honey bees. A robin will discard the sting before crushing the head and swallowing it whole. This precaution seems typical. The exception to the general rule is the honey buzzard, a scarce summer visitor, which is a specialist bee-eater, probably immune to the venom. It may be that the close-fitting feathers around the honey buzzard's head act as a protective barrier. He also eats a great number of grubs, which don't sting!

Tits spend much time searching the foliage of trees for caterpillars. Many other birds find food in, on and around trees. Nuthatches, tree-creepers and woodpeckers are able to explore the cracks and crevices of the vertical trunks, using their stiff tails as a third leg to brace the body as they grip tight with their claws. They are able to work right-side-up or upside-down, as their probing beaks search for insects and grubs. The greater spotted woodpecker has a beak which can also serve as a chisel, propelled by a tough skull which can absorb the repeated shocks as the bird penetrates the wood to reach a grub chamber. In addition to the chiselling facility, it has a long pointed tongue which is able to venture into likely holes and to spear prey with the aid of tiny barbs at the tip. This is a species which has benefited, at least temporarily, from the spread of Dutch elm disease, since the dead and dying elms are providing a feast of extra food.

Green woodpeckers also have long tongues; indeed, they are extraordinarily long. These birds of open parkland have colourful plumage which often persuades people that they must hail from some exotic clime. They specialize in insects, particularly ants, which they find in the grassy soil. The sinuous and flexible tongue is extended into an ant gallery, where the ants and pupae stick to the saliva-covered surface and are withdrawn into the open gape.

Blackbirds and song thrushes also hunt over grassy lawns but they have an entirely different approach to their prey: they indulge in a tug-o-war with the worms. First, though, they have to come to grips with their victim, which presents a problem when the worm is not anxious to advertise itself. The birds hunt by sight, since, so far as we know, worms do not make any sounds. Superficially it *looks* as though the bird is hunting by sound, because it tends to cock its head sideways in that posture which reminds us exactly of people 'listening' but, of course, as mentioned earlier, their eyes are where our ears would be.

A blackbird's eyes function quite differently from those of an aerial hunter, like an eagle. Its prey is slow-moving and close at hand, though well-camouflaged and in hiding, so the blackbird has rather flat eyes, set on each side of the head, with a wide field of vision. This gives it a safety-conscious, all-round view, which makes it difficult for predators to creep up without being seen. One section of the eye is densely packed with light-sensitive cells, so the bird cocks its head to one side to bring the grass at its feet into view, bringing that most perceptive eye section into play. (Bird eyes fit tightly in their sockets; if a bird wants to swivel its eye, it must swivel its whole head.) Working the lawn in zig-zag fashion, the blackbird simply keeps a sharp eye open for a worm posterior in a likely hole. Worms come out of their burrows in the damp night air and retreat underground as

Above: In spring blue tits may attack buds, but they also eat vast quantities of caterpillars. They hawk for honey bees, carefully removing the sting before they eat the meat

Left: Swallow.

Birds need water both for bathing and drinking. Swallows (and house martins and swifts) scoop from the surface of a pond as they flash by.

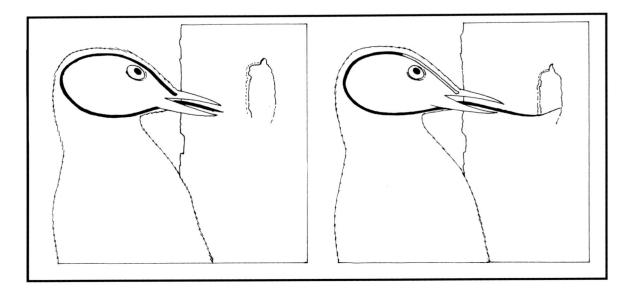

daylight approaches, so there is a great deal of truth in the saying that it is the early bird which catches the worm.

Birds have preferences for certain foods. Blackbirds much prefer worms and have been seen to throw up a cropful of soft fruit in order to make room for a juicy earthworm. They may be computer-programmed at birth to eat certain things, within the limitations of their anatomy, but they are well able to learn preferences from experience. Indeed, if they do not learn they are likely to die. They soon know the difference between a juicy sultana and a bit of stale crust! Thrushes also have a clear list of the foods they prefer. Earthworms and snails come first.

The song thrush's method of dealing with snails is effective but hardly delicate. Choosing a suitable stone for an anvil, the bird hops into the hedge or flower-border to find a specimen of its favourite snail, the colourfully-banded and camouflaged *Cepaea*. It then carries the victim to the anvil and smashes it into several pieces. Probably, it will then wipe off the slime, as it does with a slug, before eating it. Although the snail exists in a whole variety of colour and banding patterns, an individual thrush tends to select one particular version. Once it has got its eye in and settled for, say, a pink snail with four black bands, then that is the one it invariably goes for. You can confirm this by examining the broken pieces of shell around the anvil but make sure the anvil is being used by only one thrush! The thrush therefore acts as an agent

Above: Green woodpeckers have extraordinarily long tongues, sinuous and flexible, allowing them to explore deep into ant galleries and extract both ants and pupae stuck to their saliva-covered surface.

Right: Song thrushes bring snails to an 'anvil' in order to crack them open.

of evolution, encouraging the snail to produce a whole range of cryptic colour variations in self defence.

The song thrush is the only British bird to use an anvil in this way, yet there is no structural adaptation, no anatomical speciality, which gives the thrush an edge over other species. Snail meat is desirable enough for other birds as well. Opportunist blackbirds, closely related to the song thrush, often steal snails from them. Indeed, they have been observed to react to the sound of hammering at the anvil by hastening to enjoy the reward without doing any of the work. But the nearest a blackbird has been seen actually to engage in snail-bashing is when it has shaken a whole snail vigorously in a variation of the standard beak-wiping movement.

The anvil cannot be described as a tool, for the song thrush is simply taking advantage of a natural feature. The use of tools by birds is rare behaviour, confined to very few species. The classic case is that of the Galapagos woodpecker finch, which picks up a cactus spine with its beak and then uses it to extract insects from crevices and holes, but there is a promising record of a blue tit

Above: Juvenile bullfinch feeding on honeysuckle berries. In the spring its fancy may turn to fruit-tree buds, although the damage is often less serious than may be feared by gardeners.

Right: Finches have bills specially designed for cracking seeds. The delicate bill of the goldfinch (above), probes into the thistle head. The hawfinch (below) is the heavyweight of the family, able to crack a cherry stone with its nutcracker beak.

Left: Juvenile great spotted woodpecker. With its tough skull and chisel beak, this bird will be able to penetrate solid wood to search out larvae, as well as probing behind bark. Its stiff tail acts as a support in climbing.

which used an inch or so of twig to dislodge nuts in a peanut hopper when they were difficult to get at. Blue tits have long been regarded as experts at puzzles and intelligence tests because of their skill in co-ordinating beak and foot movements but the actual use of a tool is a great leap forward by an individual. Another, somewhat similar case, is recorded of a blackbird which used a forked twig, some three inches long, to brush snow away to clear a feeding space.

One technique for worm-catching is worth mentioning. Rooks, carrion crows and magpies are all partial to worms; indeed, worms are a principle item of their diet. These birds visit the edges of motorways, which are rewarding places in which to hunt. Worms are deaf but particularly sensitive to vibrations and there is some evidence to show that motorway traffic induces them to come to the surface. This happens not so much in the dry summer months but in spring and autumn, when damp conditions are favourable to the transmission of the vibrations. Apparently, high speed or badly balanced vehicles create the strongest effect. The vibrations travel farthest in the top few inches of soil, bringing worms to the surface, perhaps in the belief that there is a mole on the rampage. In order to test this theory, it was calculated that a ten-stone man stamping on a damp playing field would simulate the vibration effect of a heavy lorry travelling at 40 mph at a distance of five yards from his feet. In test conditions, the stamping did in fact persuade worms to the surface! Bait diggers wobbling their forks in damp sand on the seashore know the effect very well; so do gulls, which puddle up and down on a sandy shore for cockles and on water meadows for worms.

Gulls, like crows, are often said to eat almost anything and, indeed, that is true; nevertheless, they have well-defined preferences and worms come high on the list. There are many birds which are highly specialized in their feeding habits. The buntings, finches and sparrows are first and foremost seed-eaters. Their stout conical bills are adapted to husk or crack seeds, all the way from thistledown to cherry stones. The larger the seed, the tougher and heavier the nutcracker bill and its associated face muscles.

Seed-cracking is a fairly recent evolutionary development, dating from the time when grasses and sedges began to flourish some thirteen million years ago. From the bird's point of view, this is a sophisticated approach to feeding, since the calorific content of a seed is high and its water content low, by comparison with a caterpillar, for example. Insect-eaters must consume nearly half their body weight in a day; seed-eaters require perhaps one-tenth. Seeds present themselves in many different shapes and sizes and the finches are adapted accordingly. From the delicate probe of the goldfinch to the power-crackers of the hawfinch, each separate anatomy imposes certain limitations of choice but each, in its way, is highly successful. Watch a foraging party of goldfinches on their favourite thistles. They may be the finch lightweights but they are perfectly equipped for the job of probing into the prickly head to ease out the seeds. The sight of a charm of goldfinches attacking garden dandelions ought to be enough to convert any gardener into a dandelion fan. They approach the flowers with zest, leap-frogging on to the stems and landing about halfway up so that they weigh the head down to the ground. Then they get to work, using their long narrow bills as a pair of tweezers to probe deep into the seed-head.

The formula is the same for all the finches; only the size and power of the cracking device varies. The length, depth and width of the mandibles is designed to suit the size and hardness of the seeds the birds eat. All have grooves inside the bill which first locate the seed; then, the tongue rotates it as

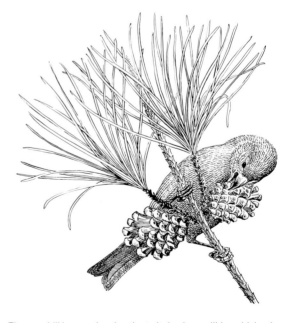

The crossbill has overlapping tips to its beak mandibles which prise the pine scales apart to reveal the oil-rich seed.

the mandibles crush. The husk peels off, leaving the kernel to be scooped up with the tongue. Each species has its preferred food and the goal is the greatest feeding efficiency in terms of calories and time. Hawfinches are even able to crack cherry stones and, if you have ever tried that yourself, you will know how tough they are.

One of the finches has a special adaptation of the bill which allows it to penetrate the fastnesses of a pine cone in order to extract the seeds. The crossbill has overlapping hooked tips to its mandibles which fully justify its name. These crossed tips serve the bird perfectly in its task of parting the reluctant pine or spruce scales to reveal the seed to its tongue. The birds are so highly specialized that our crossbills, part of a population feeding on Scots pine, have larger bills than those working the relatively easier cones in the Eurasian belt of spruce forests.

Crossbills are uncommon birds, except when they have had a particularly successful breeding season on the Continent and, in ranging far and wide in the search for cones, invade Britain in large numbers. But another close relation of the finches is an acquaintance, if not friend, of us all; that is the house sparrow. The sparrow is a seed-eater which threw in his lot with man many centuries ago; when farmers first broke and tilled the soil to produce cereal crops, he moved in to help eat the seeds. In effect, they are parasitic on us, sharing in the fruits of our labours in cultivation and urbanization. They eat at the same table and their success story runs parallel with our own. They share our failures, too. When men desert an unprofitable farm or a remote island, the sparrows shortly follow. Enjoying the farmer's corn, it made sense to share his house as well, so sparrows moved in and nested conveniently close to the dinner table. When the poultry were fed, the sparrows joined in. The warmth and safety of buildings suited them very well, so sparrows flourished as man flourished and, as villages grew into towns and cities, sparrows quickly became accustomed to the new possibilities. They also took their share of the vast quantities of straw and grain that were available for man's main transport animal, the horse.

With easy pickings all year round, there was never any need to indulge in dangerous activities like migration. Sparrows became sedentary birds, enjoying an easy life, but were never much loved. When the farmer's wife put down corn for the pigeons and poultry, she begrudged the share taken by the sparrow, from whom she got nothing in return but a lot of noisy chirrups. Then sparrows faced a setback with the invention of the internal combustion engine. With the decrease in town-stabled horses, they inevitably suffered from the loss of feed-corn. They are still less common in city centres than they were at the turn of the century but as one door closed another opened and, with the rise of suburbia and its gardens, the town sparrows flourished again. As skilled free-loaders, they enjoy lunchtime sandwich corners in the city and bird-table food in the suburb. They are not particularly welcome on the bird table but it seems that they do not require to be loved. Operating in pugnacious gangs, they terrorize other small birds and take what they want by brute force and sheer numbers.

In spring, finches and sparrows, too, have an unfortunate tendency to eat the newly-emergent buds on fruit trees, nipping them off neatly at the base. A bullfinch may deal with more than thirty in a minute and, if undisturbed, may strip a tree completely but that is an extreme case. Mostly, the damage is not so serious and, however unlikely it may sound, the actual yield of the tree in terms of fruit may be unaffected. As many as half the buds on a tree may be taken without decreasing the yield. Plums and pears are the birds' first choice, then gooseberries and currants, and it seems they know their favourite varieties. Apart from enclosing the trees or bushes in a cage, there is not much you can do about it. Fireworks have an effect for a short period. Growing some crab apples and hawthorn in your hedges may serve to distract them. In commercial fruit-growing areas, trapping may be the most effective answer. The key to the problem lies in the availability of ash seeds in winter. When there is a good crop, the bullfinches are diverted from attacking fruit buds.

No gardener will need to be reminded that sparrows attack his spring show of crocuses. There is a clear scale of colour preferences in this activity. These colour preferences extend to flowers and fruits which birds enjoy in general. Red and crimson are the favourites, followed closely by orange and yellow. Blues, whites, blacks and browns are less sought-after.

In exchange for what might seem an orgy of destruction, these small birds pay a fair price for their food. Their droppings enrich the soil with nitrogen, phosphate, potash and lime in generous quantities. Finches scatter some seeds a short distance; other seeds will pass unharmed through

the bird's stomach to be deposited far from the parent plant. When the blackbird eats a berry, in due course it voids the seed encased in a capsule of fertilizer (long before seedsmen patented the technique) some distance away. So plants spread and explore new country. Larger birds may provide long-distance transport. Ducks carry seeds, sticking to their plumage, thousands of miles, to be sown in alien pastures when they preen. Some plants, such as the common reed *Phragmites*, may owe their nearly world-wide distribution to the activities of waterfowl.

Other seeds may be deliberately planted by birds, though their motive is not that of the gardener. In autumn, when hazel nuts are plentiful, nuthatches will collect and hide them in secret places, under tree bark or in herbaceous borders, hoping to find them again in winter, when nuts are not easy to come by. This compulsion to store superfluous food is typical of the crow family. Jays are particularly enthusiastic collectors of acorns when an oak tree is heavily loaded. They eat great quantities before they begin the systematic transport of large numbers which they store in carefully chosen grassy glades, maybe a fair distance from the tree. They dig the acorn firmly into the soil, tapping it down and covering it from view. Later, in the hard times of deep winter, they take advantage of this reserve, knowing perfectly well the location of the hiding place, retrieving the acorns even when the ground is covered by snow. Not all the seeds are recovered, of course, and over

Above: In the autumn blackbirds enjoy *Cotoneaster* and firethorn berries. They digest the flesh but return the seeds to the ground, suitably covered in fertilizer.

Right: Kestrel chicks hatch in late May. The hunting male kills small birds and voles which the female dismembers and feeds to the nestlings.

the centuries many mighty oaks have owed their planting to a hoarding jay. It is one way in which an oak may reproduce itself *up* the hill!

Crows are big-brained birds and they make good use of their learning capacity. Catholic in taste, they indulge in a wide variety of seeds, fruits and animal foods. They are aggressive hunters, which actively chase small birds in flight or scatter a brood of ducklings in the hope of isolating one from its parents. They will mob herons to persuade them to disgorge fish and they will harry young herons on their first hesitant flights in the hope of causing them to crash land and provide a dinner.

There is a whole range of birds whose prime purpose is to prey on those smaller than themselves. Small birds have a lively awareness of the problem. They do not much like any flying shape which passes above them. When everything goes quiet in the garden, it is usually because a sparrowhawk passed by. Song will be hushed; the only cries will be the short sharp calls of alarm. The hawk is a master hand at carrying off any tit or sparrow which stays out in the open and animals are well aware of their likely predators. The knowledge is innate, programmed in at birth. They know which ones to ignore and which to run from.

Jays collect acorns from heavily-laden oaks in the autumn and carry them to carefully-chosen grassy places where they hide them underground to provide a food-store when times are hard. Not all the acorns are rediscovered, so some become mighty oaks.

If in doubt, they run. A robin cringes when a sparrowhawk flies by but takes no notice of a goose. The sparrowhawk is likewise programmed and has a built-in search image. For example, he might go for blue tits all the time because instinct tells him that blue tits are for catching. The female sparrowhawk, bigger and more ferocious than the male, will tackle a woodpigeon twice its own weight. The method of dealing with the victim is characteristic of a bird of prey. First, the head is bitten off and the brain is eaten; presumably it is regarded as a delicacy. The liver and lungs are enjoyed next and then the feathers are plucked so that the hawk can get at the plump breast muscles. The stomach and intestines are usually left untouched.

After that catalogue of feasting, it may seem that the birdwatcher was best served by the old-style gamekeeper who shot every hawk on sight, thus preserving the lives of their innocent prey. But in real life things are not so simple. Sparrowhawks have been eating sparrows and blue tits for millions of years and yet representatives of both species are still with us in fair numbers. For a start, the sparrowhawk does not always get his sparrow; he does not kill with every attack. Inevitably, he catches the sparrow which was slowest off the mark in getting out of the way, thereby improving the stock of the sparrows left behind. It is, of course, not in the predator's long-term interest to reduce the population of his prey species. The relationship between the hunter and his quarry is an entirely healthy one in nature. If we reduce the number of predators by shooting or by any other unnatural means, the prey species may enjoy a temporary increase but pressures such as disease, parasites, food shortages or an entirely new predator will certainly bring its numbers under control. When the sparrowhawk takes the blue tits from a bird table under your very nose, it is best to adopt a tolerant attitude. Content yourself with the knowledge that there are always more tits than hawks. Predators need a much larger hunting territory than their prey. Insects will always be more common than shrews and shrews will always be more common than owls. Natural checks maintain healthy populations.

Most birds of prey are diurnal. Some work open country, like the eagle, with its sole hunting rights to vast acreages of moorland; some, like the sparrowhawk, hunt in the intimacy of woods and hedgerows. But the owls hunt mostly at night. Although owls and the other birds of prey are not closely related, they all share some characteristics: compact hooked bills, curved talons and a taste for red meat. Those built for work over open spaces have streamlined and pointed wings. The peregrine is the supreme example of this; its swept-back wings are designed to reduce drag and maintain stability in a dive which may reach a speed of 80 mph when it is stooping on a pigeon. The sparrowhawk has short, rounded wings, of low aspect ratio, for patrolling hedgerows and woodland. These give plenty of manoeuvrability allied to short bursts of high-speed chasing and pouncing around the tree-trunks, making best advantage of surprise. Harriers quarter their fields with methodical persistence and buzzards wheel and circle at a fair height, quietly watching with high-power binocular eyes.

Peregrines are not everyday, familiar birds for many of us, sadly, and neither are falcons such as the hobby, that master aviator which can actually outmanoeuvre a swallow on the wing. But there is one falcon which has become familiar both in the city and, above all, on the motorway verges. The kestrel is the commonest of our birds of prey; it can be seen on any day, winnowing above a scrap of waste ground, both eyes firmly on the look-out for a vole. It holds a static position in the air, even when a fresh breeze is blowing, while the endless stream of high-speed vehicles passes by on the motorway. The kestrel's particular talent is achieved through the use of the otolith in its middle ear, which provides a balance mechanism that sends instructions to the wing and tail muscles; these respond to changes inducing pitch, roll and yaw. While the bird's control surfaces move freely, its head remains rock steady. In effect, it carries a perch with it in the open air and is able to scrutinize one potential food area after another. Once a vole is spotted, it is a moment's work to spill the air from its wings, plunging feet first to grasp and lock on to the prey. If voles are plentiful, there may be several kestrels at work in the same patch, since each claims only a small territory around its nest site. If voles are scarce, then the kestrels will turn their attentions to small birds. In London, they specialize in house sparrows and starlings, sometimes patronizing a starling roost to find their dinners. One young starling or two average-sized voles provide their food requirements for the day.

The kestrel's preference for voles has made it welcome in the farmers' fields. In Holland, kestrels have long been encouraged by the provision of

Peregrines have a taste for red meat. They stoop on their prey, a woodpigeon in this case, in a power-dive which may reach a speed of 80mph.

Right: Osprey bringing fish to the nest. While the female is tending young, the male may bring as many as half-a-dozen fish each day. Plunge-diving, it specializes in surface species, taking trout and pike from fresh-water lakes at breeding time, and mullet and bass while at the coast in winter. On occasion the male may pass fish to the female while both are in flight.

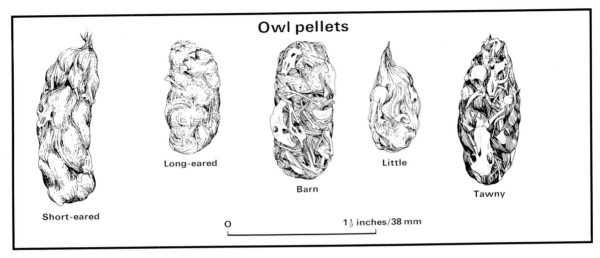

Owl pellets

Short-eared

Long-eared

Barn

Little

Tawny

0   1½ inches/38 mm

Many birds produce pellets, but owls are perhaps the best known. They usually swallow their prey whole. After digesting the flesh, the indigestible remains of the voles or small birds are regurgitated as compact pellets. Teased apart, they reveal much.

nestboxes, which increase their populations mightily. While they need open pasture or arable land over which to hunt, they need some trees or a cliff or quarry face in which to nest and it may be that this is a species whose numbers are to a certain extent controlled by the availability of nest sites in the terrain of countries like Holland. Broadly speaking, however, it is the availability and quantity of food which controls the numbers of a species.

If, for some reason, there is a super-abundance of food, then predators will do well. In some years, voles will be so successful that they reach plague proportions. These are the seasons in which short-eared owls may be able to bring up an extra brood of young but, once this increased number of owlets has been raised, they will be in trouble when the vole supply returns to normal. Then, they will have to travel hopefully, looking for fresh landscapes to conquer. The famous snowy owls in Shetland presumably arrived there as a consequence of this kind of pressure.

Owls are particularly well adapted to take over the night shift when most of the falcons and hawks have gone to roost. With their superb vision and hearing and their velvety wings, they are masters of the quiet approach to the fateful meeting of claws with bundles of meat and fur. Since small mammals prefer to show themselves only in poor light, this is the time when there are more mice and voles about. But even the roosting tawny owl is not

above the occasional sortie during the day to pick a small bird off the ground, so small birds do well to mob a roosting owl, thus bringing it to everyone's attention and diminishing its prospects of success.

Like all birds of prey, owls are particularly attentive to their young, tearing bite-sized strips of flesh off the prey and offering them to the eager gape. The adult owls, however, bolt their voles whole, though they will probably have crushed the skull first and may sometimes discard the head completely. When feeding on birds, they will pluck the wing and perhaps the tail feathers, before bolting the rest. Since their stomach juices are not very good at digesting the bones, feather and fur, these parts are ejected in due course in the form of a neatly packed pellet. Owls tend to have favourite spots on which to perch, so these pellets pile up in quite large numbers. They contain a great deal of information for the ornithological detective. Bones, skulls and teeth are firmly embedded in the furry or feathery pellets. By soaking them in water and teasing them apart, it is possible to piece together a list of the species on which the particular owl has been feeding.

There are pitfalls in this detective work. It is not only owls which produce pellets and many pellets contain no bones at all, even when the manu-facturer of the pellet has disposed of several small mammals. This is not because some birds have more powerful enzymes than others; it has less to do with their digestion than with their feeding procedure. Owls swallow their prey more-or-less whole, as already described: a complete mouse or an entire sparrow. The bones and the furry or feathery bits get thrown up as pellets in due course. But not all birds of prey swallow their victims whole. Buzzards, for example, do not swallow whole rabbits; they rip them to manageable pieces with their hooked beaks and curved claws. They eat furry pieces of meat but not the bones, so their pellets will be made up of grey fur and perhaps the odd small piece of bone.

More than 300 species of bird eject pellets. Robins and starlings, crows and waders and seabirds all use this convenient way of disposing of indigestible remains. Curlew pellets may have crab claws and bits of marine snail shell in them. But we must be careful in interpreting remains. For example, heron pellets are thoroughly misleading. We *know*, by direct observation, that their diet consists mainly of fish, eels and frogs but their pellets consist mainly of compacted fur and reveal only the bones and teeth of the water voles and moles they have eaten. This is because they have powerful digestive juices which deal with the fish bones. Pellets often need to be taken with a pinch of salt in determining a bird's main diet!

Pellets may, however, on occasion, reveal some very precise information about a bird's meals. Sometimes they contain little metal rings, which have been attached to birds' legs by scientists who want to follow their movements and find out how long they live. A buzzard's pellet was once found to contain a yellowhammer's ring, for example. Naturally enough, most of the records are from owl pellets, which have been exhaustively studied. From tawny owl pellets, rings have been found that proved to be the last remains of swallow, blue and coal tits, song thrush, blackbird, robin, pied wagtail and many other garden birds. Barn owl pellets have contained song thrush, blackbird, starling, linnet and house sparrow rings. Little owl pellets have produced much the same sort of list.

Small mammals and small birds provide the major source of food for birds of prey but there is one raptor which has specialized as a fisherman. Ospreys are specially equipped to pounce and plunge into lochs and creeks to grasp surface fish. Their fourth toe, like that of the owls, turns backwards or forwards and, in gripping the fish, the bird opposes two claws against the other two. All the toes have spines on their undersides, which further help the bird to keep a firm hold on a slippery fish.

Ospreys are capable of lifting trout or mullet weighing several pounds but other fishermen are less ambitious. Kingfishers sometimes use a hovering and plunging technique somewhat similar to that of the osprey but mostly they content themselves with perching on a suitably placed branch before hurtling into a plung-dive for a small fish. They prefer the slow-moving waters of a placid stream or river, while in autumn and winter they are common enough along the wooded shores of an estuary or sheltered sea bay. If your garden pond is near to their territory, you may even be lucky enough to have one which will rid you of the unsuitable goldfish which stir up the quiet life of your pond-dwellers.

The dipper finds its food on the rocky bed of a fast flowing stream. Using wings and feet, it flies underwater and strides about the bottom looking for eggs and larvae.

If the stream or river is more boisterous and you live away from the east and south-east of Britain, then you may see the dipper about his business. He looks a bit like a monster wren, though with black plumage and a striking white breast, but his manner of feeding is wholly different from that of the wren. His feet are those of a typical songbird but he strides about underwater, covering the ground on the stony bed of fast-flowing streams. Though his feet are not webbed, the dipper swims well, paddling hard both with what appear to be wholly inadequate feet and wings. Searching along the bottom, he picks off fish eggs and insect larvae, as well as the odd crayfish.

Herons sometimes fish from the bankside, necks stretched forward, leaning over the water, half-relaxed and half-watchful, or they may set off into shallow water, up to their thighs, wading in a

Herons hunt most effectively by slow-motion stalking. Small prey are swallowed on the spot but large fish or difficult eels may be taken to safer ground to be dealt with.

leisurely manner. This active stalking seems to be the most successful technique and it results in a fair number of attacks. The slow stalk may sometimes develop into a quick dash, with wings half open to keep the bird's balance. If necessary, the heron may even swim into deep water. The adult birds establish their individual fishing territories, spaced out along the water's edge, just as fly fishermen jealously guard their expensive water. Juvenile birds get the least productive stretches and may have to work longer hours to get a satisfactory catch. On an estuary, flounders are the most important prey, followed by eels and gobies; the best fishing is during the low-water period and on a rising tide.

Small fish are swallowed without delay. Larger ones will first be stabbed with the powerful pointed beak, then taken ashore to be killed by a back-breaking shake. Eels may well need a good deal of attention before they are dead and sometimes a flounder may be so large that the bird has to abandon it. But the heron is a versatile operator, able to deal with the most recalcitrant fish and prepared to fall back on a bit of scavenging if the fishing is poor.

Provided they have achieved a full belly, the birds will retire during the high-water period, when their working area is too deeply covered. At this time, they will be more sociable, gathering in the middle of a large grass field, perhaps, to indulge in communal preening and roosting. If

they have been battling with eels, they may well spend the best part of an hour powdering the slime on the plumage and combing it away with their special toothcomb claws.

Herons share the tidal mud of an estuary with a whole host of other birds. From autumn through to late winter, there will be wild ducks and gulls and waders in enormous numbers, with cormorants and seasonal visitors like terns and the odd osprey. These tidal regions, where the sediment-rich, fresh river water meets the salt sea and deposits its nutritious load to build mudbanks, provide ample feeding for all the birds, to say nothing of the fish which hunt there too. On the open sand and mudflats, the rhythmic passage of the tides brings a rich soup of plankton which nourishes astronomic quantities of worms and shellfish. Winkles, other seashells and various shrimp-like creatures inhabit the soft surface layer; cockles, clams, ragworms and lugworms each live at their chosen depth underneath the surface; molluscs extend their syphons to the surface to filter food from the passing current; worms migrate vertically, feeding from the current then withdrawing gracefully downwards when the tide ebbs away; under any stones or weedy places lurk shore crabs and sandhoppers.

However retiring is the creepy or crawly worm, the crustacean or shell, there will be a bird beak designed to discover it. Waders find their food by a judicious combination of touch, taste, sight and probe. Their bills have a mass of sensory nerve endings and they work their chosen level with confidence. The bills of waders come in an

Standing still, the oystercatcher probes the patch of sand in front of it, searching for molluscs. If it fails, it moves on another pace.

When the cockle is revealed, the oystercatcher's powerful bill soon breaks the valves apart and chisels out the meat.

astonishing variety of shapes, so that a whole range of different species can live off the same mudflat because they hunt at different times, different depths and in subtly different habitats. Watch the curlew stroll over the mud, pausing every now and then to probe for a ragworm. He may even run a few yards if he sees a flicker of syphon movement. With his long slender bill, he can reach down six inches into the soft mud, deep enough to find a large bivalve, which he can swallow whole. The curlew has sharp eyesight and may catch the tail end of a lugworm as it surfaces to cast its load of sand and excreta. On the upper shore, the curlew may hunt the shore crabs. Like the herons, he will retire before high water, possibly to a well-regarded and undisturbed patch of saltmarsh, where the vegetation will be beaten flat by the coming and going of many webbed feet. There he will preen and, in due course, throw up the pellet of indigestible food remains, complete with snail shell and crab legs. Sometimes he will fly to a suitable grass field and carry on hunting, this time for earthworms and larvae, in the manner to which he is accustomed during the breeding season, when he lives far from the estuary.

Curlews do not normally feed at night but other waders may have to, to fulfil their daily needs. Redshanks, which are said to peck for food as many as 40,000 times in a day, haunt tidal pools on the water's edge, jabbing and probing for shells, worms and shrimps close to the surface. Godwits and plovers all spread across the fertile mud, advancing upon the hapless small creatures like an avenging army. The myriad flocks of knot work in a sewing-machine motion with a rapid up and down movement as they advance firmly across the wet expanse. With their short bills, they are taking the small tellins off the surface.

Dunlin, the most numerous of all waders, prefer wet mud, especially close to the waterline. They peck for sandhoppers, small shells and worms. More than a quarter of a million dunlin winter in Britain. Avocets, wintering in a total number not much above the hundred, are the most sought-after by birdwatchers and the most graceful of all waders. You know them at once when you see them. No other British bird carries that long and delicate up-curved bill. It is a lively, volatile species with a seemingly inexhaustible interest in the world around it. A party of sociable avocets will take to the shallows and scoop their way in unison, leaning forward in vigorous pursuit of the tiny *mycid* shrimps. Scything the softest surface mud, they sieve the tiny shrimps and worms. Although

61

their colouring is mainly black and white, their black cap is very elegant and they have a brilliant red eye and long legs of blue-grey. Their glory is in their beak and in their dancing motion. No other birding quite matches a successful avocet watch.

As the incoming tide creeps over the mud, the birds crowd together in the last feeding place to be covered. First, the short-legged dunlin and redshank fly off to find a safe roost; then, the plovers and godwits leave, while the shelducks and avocets and gulls ride out the high-water period, swimming and socializing on the water.

Where the estuary water finally meets the sea, a new bird scene reveals itself. If there are open sand-flats, then there will be more gulls but this is the country for birds like sanderlings and the oystercatcher, a robust black-and-white wader with a long, strong, orange-red bill and pink legs. An excitable, almost nervous-seeming bird, it is quick to pipe a warning 'peep-peep' if you invade its patch. Not so common in the middle section of an estuary, this is the typical bird of the coastal cockling flats but there will be oystercatchers wherever there are cockles, especially where the cockles congregate in such numbers that their shells are at the surface. When the cockles are hidden out of sight, the bird walks a pace, then probes rapidly into the sand several times in a fanning action. If no contact is made, he moves another pace and fans again. This leaves a characteristic trail of footprints and conical holes in the sand which may persist for some time if the sand is stable enough. The bird detective may be

Above: Common sandpiper battling with a ragworm. Waders like this find their food by a combination of touch, taste and sight. Their bills have a mass of sensory nerve endings.

Left: When the tide is in, waders, like these knot, retreat to a safe roosting place, waiting for their feeding grounds to uncover again. Knot typically gather together in close-knit flocks.

63

quite certain about the events that occurred, even if there is no sign of the perpetrator.

Once the oystercatcher has located a cockle, he drives his powerful bill between the valves of the mollusc and twists them apart. Sometimes he goes for the direct assault, hammering until the shell simply breaks apart, to reveal the plump muscle inside. The oystercatcher uses similar methods on mussel beds in shallow water, stalking and jabbing at the mollusc while it is relaxed and in the feeding position, valves apart in invitation, then chiselling and scissoring at the meat. If the tide is out and the mussel closed, the bird will tear it from its anchorage and take it to a hard patch of sand, turning it until its relatively weaker flat ventral surface is exposed to the battering ram of the bird's beak. Further up the shore, around rock pools and weedy places, the oystercatcher searches for such delicacies as dogwhelks and periwinkles, which he deprives of their meaty interiors. Even limpets succumb to the direct assault; the bird carefully chooses the largest available and attacks the anterior end, the one most likely to collapse.

Turnstones are attractive and confiding birds, so effectively camouflaged that you may almost stumble on top of them as they work busily over a pile of rotting seaweed on the strandline of a beach. This one is picking off titbits in the backwash of a gentle wave.

Along the weedy and litter-strewn strandline, at the high-water mark, there are rich pickings for turnstones, jaunty birds with orange feet and bills yet so cryptically coloured in their plumage that there may be dozens of them working almost at your feet before you realize they are there, until they lift off with a metallic twittering only to land again to feed busily a few score yards away. Not surprisingly, in view of their names, they are specialists at turning weed and small stones in order to expose the sandhoppers and small fry hiding in the damp places. Crabs, winkles, sandhoppers and sandwich ends are all grist to the turnstones' mill. They may even search the decks of a trawler newly returned from fishing in the hope of picking up trawl offal and 'trash' which has escaped the hosing session or is entangled in the fishing nets. Then, replete, they may stay to roost along the gunwales, shoulder to shoulder, in the glare of the dockside lights.

Turnstones are not the only birds to enjoy foraging along the tidelines. A surprising number of passerines find worthwhile pickings among the storm-tossed debris. Many kelp flies breed in rotting seaweed, supporting a healthy population of sandhoppers, so pied wagtails, starlings, robins, sparrows and crows all come down to the shore to join the specialists like turnstones and rock pipits.

Herring gulls and black-backed gulls are the typical scavengers of the shore. Given the chance, they will always allow other birds to do the hard work; herring gulls are adept at snatching the cockle or mussel from an oystercatcher after it has gone to the trouble of opening it. If they find a mollusc by their own efforts, they are faced with a real problem, since their beaks are not high-powered enough for the job of opening it themselves. Instead, they carry the shellfish up to a fair height and then drop it on a suitable rock or roadway, to crack it open. They use this technique to prise a hermit crab from its whelk-shell.

Gulls have been quick to exploit the abundant supplies of food provided by agriculture and by some of man's more wasteful activities. Rubbish tips, sewage farms and fish quays support ever-growing numbers of birds, who also enjoy the bread and cake handouts from bird lovers. Fishing boat operations involve vast quantities of offal and 'waste' fish which sustain many seabirds, mostly herring gulls and their sea-going relations, the kittiwakes. Great black-backed gulls, fulmars and gannets benefit as well. I remember a night spent purse-seining on a vessel out of Ullapool, when we netted seventy tons of mackerel in the Minch and a whirling snowstorm of gannets came to claim their share. One way and another, twenty species of birds have been recorded scavenging from trawl nets, either as they break the surface or from the dead and dying organisms which floated free or from the quantities of 'trash' which were hosed through the scuppers after the catch was sorted. Mostly, this 'trash' consists of undersized whiting and similar fish, along with a random mixture of dabs and sprats, shellfish and crustaceans, depending on the trawl depth. If cod and saithe are gutted at sea, then the offal is tossed overboard, to be enthusiastically taken by fulmars, which are especially keen on the rich livers.

Not surprisingly, since plant food in the plankton requires specialized harvesting, most seabirds are carnivorous. The 'seagulls' are, after all, mostly coastal birds which find a good deal of their food inland; they are naturally omnivorous. There are perhaps a dozen bird Families in all which make a living from the sea. Most are more-or-less coastal, especially the gulls, though the kittiwake is a sea-going gull. Of the gulls, terns, petrels, auks and gannets, relatively few species are truly pelagic but the rewards of a seafaring life are real. The North Atlantic current carries a cargo of plankton riches from sub-arctic waters, a great bounty supporting vast stocks of fish around our shores. There is no shortage of prey for the birds which are equipped to catch it. The seafaring life is hard in terms of weather conditions but relatively safe from predators. As a result, sea-going birds have an enviable tendency to long life.

Fishing methods vary. Gannets plummet into the sea and plunge-dive from as much as 100 feet (30 m) up in pursuit of mackerel and herring. The fearful impact is cushioned by the shock-absorbing breast plumage and by air-sacs under their skin. They also have particularly strong skulls. Their nostrils are conveniently placed inside the mouth to avoid the uncomfortable effects of water jetting inside them. On occasion, skuas may pursue and harass them, taking the captured fish in an act of piracy. Indeed, skuas will chase any seabird in possession of a desirable catch.

Kittiwakes may also feed by plunge-diving, though in a far less spectacular manner, since they do not close their wings at the last moment as gannets do. Kittiwakes also pick fish and plankton from the surface in a sort of dipping action and are enthusiastic followers of fishing boats. Fulmars, too, have benefited enormously from the increase in fishing vessels and fishing activities. Ever since the heyday of whaling, they have taken advantage of the offal rejected by fishermen and, over the last hundred years and more, the trawling industry has helped them to colonize the whole of the British coast. They also take natural food, dipping in the manner of the kittiwakes.

Terns fish in the manner of a sea-going kestrel, hovering, often at the very edge of the sea, and dropping like a stone to recover just before impact and to pick their sand-eels from the surface.

While gannets penetrate only a very short distance underwater, other birds indulge in active diving in pursuit of their quarry, reaching deep down to as much as fifty fathoms (90 m) in the case of auks. In order to become successful divers, certain birds have undergone some modifications

FOOD AND FEEDING

The local rubbish tip provides good birdwatching! Crows and gulls especially welcome the choice morsels delivered daily.

Terns fish in the manner of a sea-going kestrel, hovering, often at the very edge of the sea, before dropping to pick off sand eels. Here a fresh fish is brought to the hungry chick.

to their anatomy and physiology, although in one way their skeletons are in a sense more directly related to their reptilian ancestors. They lack the hollow, airy bone structure of most birds, thus increasing their specific gravity and improving underwater performance. Before diving, they actually reduce volume by breathing out air, relying underwater on oxygen from the muscle and not from the respiratory system. They also have the facility to compress their contour feathers in such a way that less air is trapped against the body; this reduces undesirable buoyancy. Sea ducks like the scoters also use this facility to reduce buoyancy and to adopt a low-profile posture if they are alarmed.

Scoters tend to work close in to the shore in sheltered waters, perhaps not in depths of more than about five fathoms (9 m), searching for molluscs on the bottom, but razorbills, guillemots and puffins are superb submariners, the northern hemisphere version of the penguin. Using both wing and foot paddles, they actively chase sand-eels and sprats through the open water. During the breeding season, they naturally work within commuting distance of the remote islands where they breed but for most of the year they range far out into the Bay of Biscay and round to the Mediterranean. Puffins, especially, are deep-sea sailors, spending the winter far from shore in the North Atlantic, but what they feed on at this time is largely a matter of conjecture.

Cormorants and shags are inshore divers, though they are hardly in competition with each other. The shag is decidedly a marine fisherman and the cormorant mainly an estuary and fresh-water fisherman. Although the subjects of a good deal of envy by, and irritation to, human fishermen, who seem to object to the fact that the cormorant is better at the job than they are, both birds eat mainly non-marketable and non-sporting fish.

Cormorants seem to lead enviably idle lives, perched on some post or mooring buoy for hours on end, but when they finally go to work they are

energetic. They jack-knife in a manner that puts an olympic swimmer to shame and they may remain underwater for some time, emerging suddenly with the best part of an eel wrapped around their necks. Sometimes the eel may be longer than the cormorant. Flatfish and dabs are their main prey and they may take several in quick succession, some so large that it is quite a struggle to swallow them. The cormorant is well designed for the job. Its tongue has a rasping surface which inclines towards the throat, so that the fish can only go one way. If the fish is a big one, it may be shaken about and even thrown in the air but it will always be arranged so that it is swallowed head first. Like its relative the pelican, the cormorant has a roomy throat-pouch to receive the fish. The gullet is a long flabby tube capable of great expansion, so that, while the flatfish is sliding gently down, the birds neck may look like a balloon. For all that, the cormorant has no difficulty in breathing and there is no danger that it will choke. The windpipe is rather like a flexible vacuum cleaner pipe; it does not kink, even when the supple bird is twisting and turning. Unlike most water birds, the plumage of a

A juvenile cormorant paddling slow ahead to a new fishing mark. In a few moments it will up-end and jack-knife down to hunt flounders and eels on the bed of the estuary.

Cormorants use their powerful webbed feet to provide underwater propulsion. The tail and wings act as control surfaces.

cormorant becomes sodden as a result of its diving activities, which is why it spends so much time at its toilet, hanging its wings out to dry in the breeze.

Divers, gulls and seabirds in general have a particular problem when it comes to dealing with the quantity of salt which they inevitably ingest in both drinking and fishing. They absorb far more than is healthy for them and more than their renal system can deal with. The surplus salt is conveyed by a network of blood vessels into fine tubes connected with the nasal glands. This concentrated sodium chloride is in solution and drips constantly from the end of the beak. In the case of diving birds like the gannet, whose nostrils are blocked in order to avoid access to water on impact, the solution weeps into the mouth from the nasal entrance in its roof and the bird flicks it away by shaking its head. This useful facility is confined to marine birds. Passerines, for example, are unable to cope with excess salt and it is most important never to offer salted peanuts in bird-table nut-cages.

Fresh water is a vital requirement for birds, both for bathing and for drinking. This requirement

varies in different species. Some birds can last a long time without drinking, some will die within a few days but none can manage entirely without water, for it is essential to the proper functioning of their bodies. Although birds do not sweat, they

Left below: Herring gulls jostling for the offal when fish are gutted at sea.

Below: Gulls have increased their populations enormously during this century. But although various forms of man-provided rubbish have undoubtedly contributed to their success, the reasons are not entirely clear.

lose water partly by breathing but mainly by excretion and must make up the loss. They derive some of their water from food, and the rest from drinking. Swallows and swifts scoop from the surface of a pond as they flash by, as do house martins, which have also been seen to sip dew. Tree-living species may sip from foliage after rain but most birds will visit ponds and streams. They fill their bills, then raise their heads to let the water run down their throats. Pigeons are an exception to the rule, since they are able to keep their bills immersed and to suck up the water that they need.

4
Courtship

A wren proclaims his territory.

Some birds lay claim to an exclusive feeding territory over which they 'own' the rights; others mix freely. Eagles, herons and dippers maintain a fair degree of control over their most productive hunting areas by virtue of brute force. On the other hand, many species hunt co-operatively. When it comes to the all-important business of setting up a family home and reproducing themselves, different species again go about the job in a variety of different manners. The eagles remain aloof; the herons become sociable; the starlings, which enjoyed noisy sociability in autumn and winter, set up discreet family units; the gannets, which fished sociably, also nest sociably, within limits. The goldfinch claims hardly any land at all, while the tits like to call an acre their own.

Generally speaking, the ownership of a breeding territory, as opposed to a feeding territory, is most important in an individual bird's life. Feeding potential in the home patch obviously matters greatly but there are other factors to be considered; for example, the availability of a suitable nest site and security from disturbance or enemies. The prime function of a territory is to establish a home area which serves to sustain a relationship between a mated pair and provide life-support for the ensuing family. Some species, such as robins, set about the job with gusto; some, like sparrows, in a half-hearted manner; some, like rooks, do it in noisy communities. Although, in the last resort, the weapons of defence and attack are wings, beaks and claws, territorial battles are almost exclusively fought in terms of postures adopted, colours raised and songs proclaimed.

When birds have a striking ruff or crest, brilliant colouring or an unusual feature of some sort, it is almost bound to be concerned with display. The advertisement is almost always directed at members of the same species, sometimes male, sometimes female. In a few cases, both sexes assume display plumage. The great crested grebes, for example, indulge in complex water displays of head shaking and 'facing up' to each other. Both male and female sprout crests and tippets in the spring as spectacular adornments to their plumage. But in most species it is the male bird which displays colour and movement.

Feathers play an important role in bird language. Either the whole of the body plumage or individual groups of feathers may be erected or depressed at will to bring about startling changes in colour or outline. Such displays can be turned on or off very quickly by the action of the feather papillae muscles, which are similar to those that make our hair stand on end. Confidence might be communicated by sleek feathering, while a bird with its plumage fluffed out might possibly be a weak, submissive individual advertising the fact that it is not interested in a fight, but language is mostly far more specific, particularly when it comes to the signals that birds use to threaten or woo each other. In such cases, the plumage is modified to amplify its communicative function, over and above the more mundane requirements for insulation, camouflage and flying.

During the course of evolution, feathers which are involved in display tend to become changed in such a manner as to increase the impact of the performance, thereby making the feather movements more effective as signals. These, in consequence, become easier to interpret by those who see them. In other words, the message is forced across loud and clear. To another male, the signal is, 'Keep off'; to a female it reads, 'Come closer'.

Robins provide the classic example of birds which are fiercely territorial, keeping a hold on their home patch more-or-less throughout the year, but in most cases the urge to set up land ownership is connected with the increasing daylight and rising temperatures of spring. Chemical changes in the endocrine system cause the pituitary gland to release hormones which trigger the reproductive cycle. In the male, his testes increase in size and he becomes more aggressive. He proclaims his virility boldly.

Amongst the passerines, the beginning of the territorial season is the signal to burst into song but their efforts will be half-hearted unless there is someone to listen. Two rivals may sing against each other almost throughout the day, whereas an isolated and paired male may hardly bother to sing at all. The song has a job to do and, regrettably, is not primarily an expression of carefree joy.

The chaffinches, which spent the winter in exclusively male hunting parties, keeping in touch with metallic 'pink' calls, become lone hunters, polishing their individual songs both to warn off rival male suitors and to persuade a potential female to inspect the property. This is true of other species as well. Each has its own distinctive 'brand image', an identifiable song. Warblers, finches, tits, thrushes and dozens of different species each has a clearly distinctive call, conveying basic information about species, sex and land ownership status. The effect of the broadcast will depend on

In courtship display, great crested grebes face each other to 'head-shake', then indulge in a furious water chase.

who hears it. Another cock bird of the same species will recognize it as a threat; a female will hear it as an invitation, unless she is already suited. There is a world of meaning in the song, whether it is the few phrases of a chaffinch or the musical and inventive offering of a blackbird.

Display, whether of plumage or song, is a dangerous undertaking, exposing the performer and making him conspicuous to his enemies, but he must indulge in it, since there is a pressing need for the individual to breed and perpetuate his characteristics, be they good or bad. Natural selection makes the final choice but, to the individual, there is no argument about it: he wishes to be 'remembered' by his progeny.

Since the song is designed to be heard, the singer chooses a song-post with care. An experienced male will know the best place, whether it is the top of an old tree or a television aerial. Skylarks, living in the treeless open spaces, rise to an imaginary tree in the sky in order to proclaim their message. Robins will perch inconspicuously in everyday life but come out into the open to sing. Their territorial song-battling begins with the winter, when they come out of the annual moult, and

Both male and female great crested grebes have dark ear-tufts and red ruffs or tippets round the backs of their necks from early spring to late summer.

continues through till the sweeter warbling of courtship in the early months of the year. Then their singing is joined by many other birds, till gardens are full of music as well as colour.

Most of the persistent songbirds are easy to identify. 'That's the wise thrush; he sings each song twice over', wrote Browning. There are other, less obtrusive characters, who prefer to stay out of sight behind a curtain of green leaves, letting their voices do the serenading. Dunnocks, for instance, match their singing to their characters; they produce a thin, rather subdued, warble. The wren, however, although he might normally be called unobtrusive in habits, has one quality, when it comes to singing, which would get him thrown out of any choral society. He does not seem to have any control. It's difficult to credit the sheer volume produced by that tiny scrap of a bird, belting out his message in five-second bursts from somewhere in the bush. The only other small bird I can think of which goes in for maximum effect is the dipper but he *needs* to turn the volume up to overcome the splashing and gurgling of white water over the boulders of his stream. Dippers, incidentally, maintain a linear territory along a stretch of water, claiming fishing rights over perhaps a couple of miles.

While birdsong may have an almost entirely utilitarian purpose for birds, it certainly provides great pleasure for people. Of our resident British songbirds, I think the thrush family provides the quality performers. The song thrush is a real musician and plenty of people would argue that the blackbird is one of the greatest singers in the family. It performs on a boxwood flute and in two quite different styles. The early-morning song is a little half-hearted, a trifle monotonous and staccato, building to an anti-climax, but the song of evening is a vast improvement. It is longer and with more musical phrasing, a rich and mellow warble, lower in pitch than the song thrush, unforced and full of feeling. If only the blackbird could bring himself to a firmer conclusion he would be the finest singer of all.

Even when the incoming migrants come to cheer us with 'cuckooing' and 'chiffchaffing', few of the melodious warblers, even the blackcaps, can match our home-grown songsters for musicality and invention. The shy nightingale is the strongest contender for the prize; perhaps it puts our blackbird into second place on points. It is not because the nightingale sings at night, when the competition is silenced, that it is so highly

Above: Skylarks live in open country with few trees. If there is a convenient post they will be glad to sing from it.

Left: If there is no song-post, then they will mount to an imaginary tree-top in the sky to proclaim their message.

regarded, for nightingales often sing during daylight hours, when they make all other songs sound small. No bird has such power and range, such inventiveness allied with consistency.

It is easier to understand why owls hoot at dusk and in the night, since they are by very nature birds of the darkness, if not of evil omen. They tend to call most on calm, quiet nights for the good reason that sound carries farthest then and owls maintain good-sized territories. Autumn and spring are the hooting seasons, though they may call at any time. When one owl hoots, his neighbour replies and then his neighbour's neighbour and so on. In no time at all the valleys are alive with the sound of music. The low-pitched voice carries well, like a foghorn which is designed to carry its message far into the distant sea. Owls could be called the foghorn beacons of the dark wood.

Very few female birds indulge in song as a rule, although both male and female robins sing and a female wren sometimes sings with a quiet, un-wren-like voice. In the interesting case of the rare

red-necked phalarope, the male and female roles are reversed. It is the female of these waders which has the bright plumage and it is she who arrives first at the breeding territory to advertise herself by singing. The male is dowdy by comparison and, in due course, he is the one who incubates and cares for the young entirely by himself.

Both male and female cuckoos call 'cuckoo', although the male is the most assiduous; the female also voices a quieter kind of bubbly chuckle. Although their nesting arrangements are unconventional, they nevertheless establish a breeding territory. The female, who arrives after the males are already calling, chooses the area, to which she returns year after year. She homes in on the kind of country that suits the particular species of foster-parent she is programmed to victimize.

'Song' is not always musical and not always even vocal. Grouse drum with their wings, snipe use their tails and woodpeckers hammer with their

Role-reversal in birds. The female red-necked phalarope has the bright breeding plumage and she takes the initiative in courting. As in the similar case of the dotterel, she establishes the breeding territory. After laying the clutch of eggs, she leaves the male to incubate and care for the chicks. This procedure presumably allows the female to set up another family elsewhere in the care of another male, so increasing her output.

beaks. The object of these exercises is the same as the music of the songsters.

The woodpecker's chisel-like beak is designed for chipping bark, exploring dead and dying tree trunks for fat larvae and for excavating nest holes, but in establishing a territory he is interested only in making as much noise as possible. He carefully selects a branch with a powerful resonating effect, so that the tapping sound carries well. The rate of tapping is astonishingly fast: a great spotted woodpecker has tapped in a sustained burst of fourteen strikes in less than one second (counted from frames of high-speed movie film). The bird's

Robins are indefatigable in defence of their territory, and they protect it throughout the year. If it is threatened they display vigorously, swaying about as they present their fluffed-up breast feathers at the intruder.

skull is specially designed to take the strain of hammering. Spongy tissue between the bones connecting beak to cranium acts as a shock absorber.

The snipe makes its 'bleating' sound as it rockets downwards during aerial display. Its outer tail feathers are separated from the main fan and the rushing air is vibrated across a harp-like structure. Snipe are said to be known as heather-bleaters or moor-lambs, but I am bound to say that I have never actually known anyone use those names, apposite though they may be.

A golden eagle may defend a territory of more than thirty-five square miles but our garden songbirds have more modest requirements. It is possible to plot these requirements fairly accurately by close observation of marked individuals and their behaviour. The parties of tits which move about in flocks may have a working range of two or three miles in suburb and woodland but, as breeding time approaches, they separate and lay claim to a much smaller but exclusively owned area, which might be the size of a football pitch. An older, more experienced bird might well hold a larger area but not all birds manage to get a territory. There are always hopeful youngsters waiting to snap up any property which becomes vacant.

Quite apart from the obvious advantages when bringing up a family, it makes sense for a bird to be working a patch which it knows well. Some birds, like robins, stake their claims immediately after the autumn moult but it may be just before nest-

building time that a goldfinch takes up ownership and even then the defended area consists only of the few square yards around the actual nest. Both goldfinches and robins may jointly own the same country, of course, for territorial disputes only occur between males of the same species. One of the causes of the spring-time fighting on the bird table is that birds which have fed there amicably in the non-territorial days of winter now find themselves trespassing on someone else's property.

If, unusually, the warning postures and song are flouted and an intruder enters a bird's territory, then it reacts with vigour. The incumbent has a considerable advantage, knowing his ground and feeling secure in his title, and he tends to win the heated-up battle of intense posturing and display. Actual physical attack, involving risk of injury and dangerous loss of feathers, is rare. Almost always, confrontation is a case of bluff and counter-bluff. It is at their boundaries, where two neighbours both feel equally assured, that the greatest battles occur. The red breast of his neighbour acts like a red rag to a bull for any robin. He 'shows his colours', stretching up and pointing his beak to the sky with his tail cocked up, making the most of his scarlet breast but there is a great deal of fudging and backing down. The bird is torn between the urge to fight for his rights and the urge to flee the field. He may indulge in displacement activity, pulling furiously at an innocent leaf or preening extravagantly, like a worker who thumps the desk when he really wants

79

Above: Starlings in territorial combat. On occasion they will willingly fight smaller birds in order to take over a nest site.

Left: Rooks squabble incessantly at breeding time. Non-combatants will stand by in the hope of stealing a nest-twig or two while the fighters' attention is elsewhere.

Top: Chaffinch and great tit deciding dominance. This sort of encounter is unlikely to result in anything worse than hurt feelings.

Right: Gannets indulge in elaborate courtship displays. One of the components is this neck-fencing.

to thump the boss! When a bird decides that discretion is the better part of valour, he adopts a submissive posture, turning away from the victor or perhaps exposing his throat in capitulation, 'turning the cheek' and walking or flying quietly out of trouble. The victor, his ownership of land confirmed and conceded, tells the world, in song, that he is the greatest.

Chasing about the garden and shaping up for mock fights is typical blackbird behaviour. Blackbirds are not particularly sociable, although they are tolerant enough most of the time, but in late winter you often see a gathering of cock birds throwing their weight about and establishing an order of precedence, hoping to impress the hens. They parade about with tails down and wings half open, measuring their strength one against the other, even though there may not be a female in sight. Part of the game is to chase each other round the herbaceous border. Most of these battles are entirely chivalrous affairs of honour. The object of the exercise is to produce a winner and a loser, with loss of face but no loss of blood. Even a few misplaced feathers can be serious for a bird, so both sides try hard to avoid damage, but occasionally mock battles develop into the real thing. The more pugnacious contender seizes his adversary with his beak and belabours him with his wings. Mute swans are said to fight to the death but very rarely.

A curious territorial battle occurs when a bird comes face to face with himself in a mirror; perhaps it is a car wing mirror or hub-cap or a reflecting window. Finding that his spirited posturing is returned in like measure, he is even more disconcerted when, on attacking the intruder, he finds that he is beating against glass. This kind of activity may take up a great deal of wasted time and exhausting effort for a bird. Pied wagtails seem especially prone to it and it is a kindness to cover up the mirror to remove the 'threat'.

When all the land-grabbing and fighting is done and our hero has established himself as king of the castle, life is still full of difficulties. Even when a suitable female has presented herself and been chosen, the course of true love is far from clear. Courtship, as we all know, is fraught with problems. Most animals, including ourselves, tend to shy away from actual touch most of the time but perpetuation of the species requires physical contact. It is the function of the courtship ritual to overcome that natural reserve and the object of the

Faced with an 'intruder', even though it is actually its own image in a mirror, the ringed plover draws itself up to its full height, then crouches to reveal its tail feathers in intimidating display.

This pied wagtail sees what it assumes to be a rival in a car mirror, and will waste a great deal of time trying to persuade its image to go away or drop dead!

Blackcocks at the lek. While they indulge in manly displays, the females are watching from concealed positions.

ritual, no matter what the species, is to lead gently towards ever closer contact and eventual copulation.

There is much anxiety, tension and fear to cope with. The very apparatus of aggression and combat are now employed to a very different end. The screaming of land-grab becomes the language of love. The gorgeous colours of the plumage are shown off to best advantage. Ear tufts may be erected and gyrations reveal the best profile. Music and movement beguile with billing and cooing but mating is so fraught with conflicting emotions that one wonders how it ever succeeds. While the cock bird is pressing close attention on a hen, he may be distracted by a rival cock singing contentiously. He must instantly break off one kind of engagement to enter another, using the same weapons of song, dance and plumage for opposing purposes. No wonder the interval between first encounter and consummation is sometimes a long one.

Tits begin to pair while still members of the winter flock, at which time the male may actually defend a territory around the female as she moves about. At night, the flock breaks up and the birds go to roost as individuals but, in the case of a pair, the male will see the female home, perhaps singing

a goodnight song and indulging in a bit of amorous chasing before he tucks her up safely. He then retires like a gentleman, going off to roost on his own and coming back to call for her at breakfast time. In due course, the female's roost-site becomes the nest site, the centre of the feeding and breeding territory.

Pigeons press their suit with splendid aerial displays of soaring and diving, holding their wings out stiffly and clapping them loudly together. A male kestrel dives out of the sky screaming at his female, while she reacts by turning over in the air and presenting a fine, sharp set of claws to him. Once kestrels are committed to pairing, the female will be dependent on the male for food. The giving and receiving of food is an important part of the courtship process for many species (including man, of course!).

A courting pair of robins may look identical but the two birds know the parts they must play. The male's red breast of aggression becomes an instrument designed to impress and, perhaps, subdue. The female redbreast allows herself to approach timidly, then turns her head aside in a submissive manner. She quivers and crouches like a begging juvenile. The cock bird then feeds his hen a choice morsel. She accepts and is nourished both physically and maritally. The pair bond is strengthened and the sex drive is strengthened, also. The two birds can pass to closer proximity. Courtship feeding has more than token value; it

Guillemots are sociable birds, breeding in colonies on inaccessible cliff ledges. Their single egg is laid on the bare rock and it is pear-shaped to render it less likely to roll off the edge.

Right: Woodcock on the nest. Only the female incubates: she blends effectively with the dappled woodland background.

At the ceremonial 'siege', herons indulge in a slow-motion dance of courtship.

allows time for the two to get together in the context of an innocuous activity, which does not at first sight have sexual significance.

Some birds go in for a form of courtship which is almost public, though confined to their own species, of course. Blackgame are birds of the interface between woodland and moorland; they do well at the edge of newly planted conifer forests in remote areas of the Border country and Central Highlands. At courtship time, they indulge in a spectacular communal dancing display, the 'lek', which takes place in a carefully chosen grassy arena. In the first light of dawn, the male birds, the blackcocks, gather together to strut and prance, showing off their plumage to best advantage. The drably coloured females, the greyhens, stay more-or-less concealed at the edge of the arena or watch from a convenient tree top. There follows a sequence of events rather like boxing 'rounds'. In round one, the blackcocks jump and 'crow', hopping and skipping and uttering lustful cries. In round two, they dash at each other purposefully, with hoarse calls, sometimes hitting each other with a bump. In round three, they relax slightly in their 'mini-territories', craning forward with necks blown up and bills pointing down to the ground, crooning and 'rookooing'. All this time, the greyhens have been sizing up the character and physique of the males on offer. Then, in an atmosphere of high tension, a female runs into the centre of the ring, amongst the cockbirds, to become the object of immediate attention and display. In full view of the assembly, the 'master' cock, who naturally has the finest colouring and the most splendid singing voice, is united with the most attractive hens, copulating without more ado. The strongest stock therefore prevails in the best traditions of natural selection. After the lek is over, the males have nothing to do with the business of nesting, incubation or raising the family.

Social behaviour of a more conventional kind is typical of the rooks and jackdaws and many others. An established pecking order is character-istic of these communities and, although the order may be in a continual process of change, the system works well. Social breeding clearly offers many advantages, including the sharing of food resources, mutual protection from enemies and the general stimulus of 'togetherness'.

Herons, while fairly solitary outside the breed-ing season, begin to gather at a chosen standing ground not far from the communal heronry perhaps as early as Christmas but more usually in late January and February. As the days lengthen and feeding becomes easier, their endocrine systems release a surplus of chemical secretions which stimulate the sex organs and trigger colour changes in the bills and feet. The mandibles, normally yellowish, and the feet and legs, norm-ally a dull brown, flush a deep pink. Since both sexes look exactly alike, at least to us, it may be that the performance which follows serves to distinguish between them but more likely it serves to synchronize the breeding activities of the colony.

The courtship gathering of herons is known as a 'siege' (whereas in rooks it is a 'parliament'). At first there are only a few birds but numbers build up to a dozen or so; all stand quietly motionless, facing in the same direction. It is an unemotional scene, with something of the atmosphere of a gentleman's club but the stage is set for a courtship dance. One bird raises its wings, runs a few steps and skips about a bit; then, perhaps, the others will raise their wings in a half-hearted way and dance a couple of steps. The whole performance is restrained, decorous. There is no unseemly contact, no billing or cooing. It is all over in no time at all. If a new arrival flies in, the action may perk up again but it soon dies down. Days later, the males will remove themselves to take up stations in the tree-top heronry, there to posture and call a little in order to attract females. There will be some formal flights from the nest-site to review the surrounding countryside, the whole colony in close company. It is a slow-motion affair.

Aerial species such as martins and swifts, which find their food while flying in the sky, tend to nest in colonies since they have no need to 'space' themselves and corner a personal food supply. Seabirds, too, feed in social flocks over vast areas of open water and they tend to breed colonially, asking little in the way of territory beyond the freehold of a nest site. Guillemots crowd together at nest ledges on precipitous cliffs. Like the herons, although with a great deal more noise, their sociability may be a prerequisite for successful pair formation. They egg each other on. Like gannets, they keep at pecking distance from each other. They are friends with the neighbours but not too friendly. Terns, like robins, offer choice titbits to each other but they do their courtship feeding in flight, passing the ritual fish from one to the other. At the chosen nest site, they reassure themselves

Little ringed plovers, like a number of other birds, prepare no more than a saucer-shaped scrape in the sand to cradle the eggs. For all that, they are not at all easy to see.

that they are a matched pair; the male bird asserts a dominant role, the other accepts a few token pecks to confirm the relationship.

The establishment of territory and the ritual of courtship are essential preliminaries to nest building, since it is vital to have a food supply on which to rear young and no eggs will hatch unless they are the consequence of mating by a mature pair. Nests, furnished with eggs, are a reminder of the reptilian ancestry of birds. They represent a procedure which is fraught with danger yet there is no alternative, since to carry developing embryos within their bodies would hamper the birds too severely in flight. The females, accordingly, wear cunning camouflage plumage to suit their nesting habits and adopt a low profile.

The timing of nest building is critical. Birds rarely have the temerity to nest in winter, apart from a very few species which have good reasons for being exceptions to the rule. For the majority, the odds against success are high and the

evolutionary process soon eliminates the misguided. Birds born during seasons of food shortage do not survive to perpetuate the error of their parents. Natural selection determines the breeding season, just as it determines everything else, and the breeding season proper begins with the construction of a nest, or, in some cases, the repair and maintenance of a long-established construction. The job of the nest is to provide a cradle for eggs and a home for the chicks. Choosing the building site will have been a part of the courtship activity and may be decided long before construction work begins. Residents may have spent the winter searching for the best plot but summer visitors have less time to spare. They may select a site and start building on the same day. For each species, a particular site is preferred, though there will be some degree of tolerance; and each makes a particular form of structure. Carrion crows may well prefer to build in trees but on a windswept island they may have to make do with the top of a bramble bush.

Many birds occupy a hole of some sort in cliff faces or trees. One obvious advantage of these sites is a degree of protection from weather and

Inside a nesting-box. A blue tit rotates her body in order to make a warmly-shaped cup for the eggs, and the hen returns with food for a brood of twelve-day-old chicks.

predators but suitable interiors are not easy to find, which is one reason why man-made tit-boxes are so successful by comparison with the open-plan type designed for birds like robins. However, a cock great tit will work hard to find several possible nest sites before he takes his mate on a tour of inspection. She makes the final choice, displaying her pleasure with quivering wing movements. A particular site may be attractive to more than one pair of birds. Blue tits may build their nest inside a welcoming hole, only to be evicted by tree sparrows, which actually build another nest on top of that prepared by the tits, eggs and all.

Some birds of prey and some seabirds manage perfectly well without a nest at all. Some waders prepare little more than a scrape in the sand, with perhaps a pebble or two to decorate it. Swans, ducks and geese make generous nests, lined with warm feathers. Water birds like grebes and coots build floating rafts, which are anchored to a few reeds or willow shoots. If the water level rises, they add a few more inches on the top. Gannets and shags prepare a mound of gelatinous seaweed, decorated, perhaps, with odds and ends of rope, which may prove their undoing if this becomes entangled in their feet or necks. Their nests are out in the open for all to see because the site is carefully chosen for its remoteness and freedom from interference by predators. Other nests are sited with the greatest care so that they remain undetected by small boys as well as weasels and magpies.

Building materials, as in all the most harmonious houses, will be found nearby and will depend on the local vegetation and on the secondhand market. The process of collecting is part of the continuing courtship ritual and choice twigs or grasses may be presented as a reinforcement of the pair bond. It is in these early stages of nest building that you have your best chance of discovering a nest, because you will see birds struggling to get airborne with sticks and stems, on the way to the site. Much material may be wasted, for, if the main frames fall to the ground, they are often ignored by the birds, who fly off to search for replacements. In many cases, as in that of rooks, the female will stay close to the nest site to discourage stick thieves. Once the framework is stable, the bird will shape the egg cup by means of a swivelling motion, by moulding with its breast and feet. Grasses and mosses will be packed tight and the bill will be used to work in odd strands and

Nests

Rook

Great spotted
woodpecker

Long-tailed tit

Goldfinch

Ringed plover

Coot

House martin

Kittiwake

The function of a nest is to provide a cradle for eggs and a home for chicks. Each species has preferences for siting and construction.

There may be a dozen chicks inside the long-tailed tit's nest-ball. The outer construction is of moss plastered with lichen.

to keep the nest tidy. After the main structure is finished, another layer may be added; for example, a blackbird will have an inner mud layer with a lining of soft stuff, such as feathers, which provide a warm bed for the eggs. Cock wrens may build a series of outer nests but wait for their mates to make a choice before adding the soft lining to the chosen one.

The bird's bill is a tool used with great dexterity in this activity. The long-tailed tit is one of the most skilled of builders. In a bramble or gorse bush or perhaps in a fruit tree, both birds of the pair build an oval-shaped ball, with an entrance hole cunningly arranged towards the top. Wool, moss and spider's web are interwoven, with an outer wall of grey lichens. This part of the job may take nine or ten days. After a day or two's holiday, they spend a good week on an inner lining which consists of a truly staggering number of feathers, anything up to two thousand! Yet in this five-inch (13 cm) ball it seems there is room for a dozen eggs to produce a dozen fledglings. It must be wonderfully warm at night.

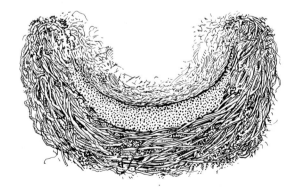

Above: Blackbirds' nests have a lining of mud with an inner lining of fine grasses.

Left: Coots nest in a clump of reeds. Their main requirement is that the site should be surrounded by water so that predators are deterred. It is well anchored to survive spring gales.

91

Goldfinches at the nest. The female incubates but both parents will feed the nestlings.

Sparrows build their untidy nests in a variety of locations. It may look scruffy, but there is a cosy interior lining of warm feathers.

Goldfinches use thistledown for their nest linings. The beaks which act as tweezers in extracting thistle seeds from deep in the flower head are equally adept at teasing out the soft snow-white down. It is typical of goldfinches that they build high up in trees and 'out on a limb' on swaying branches, away from the danger of small boys but very wind-blown. They make a specially deep nest to keep the eggs safe. The main structure is made of roots, grasses and wool and they bind it to the living twigs with spider silk. It is flexible and strong but it is a complicated affair and remains vulnerable in a gale. Goldfinch nests often take a tumble. Perhaps they were the original inspiration for the nursery rhyme, 'Hush-a-bye baby in the tree tops, when the wind blows the cradle will rock'. If the nest does blow down, the birds will start again and build another, working ten minutes to half-an-hour at a time and taking several days for the job.

By contrast, house sparrows spend no more time than they have to and make no pretence to a sophisticated nest. They make use of any available hole, provided it is reasonably close to their food supply. Tucked in under the eaves of a house or behind a drainpipe, they find a convenient niche in somebody else's house, for they like our company even if we do not much care for theirs. Their nest may be easy to see but it will always be difficult to get at and it will always be a scruffy affair.

Struggling off the ground, lugging a piece of string or straw half-a-dozen times as long as themselves, sparrows throw together a large, untidy, domed structure of hay and straw with a side entrance leading to an inner chamber lined with feathers or wool. Given half a chance, they will opt out of building altogether by taking over a blue tit's nestbox or a house martin's nest, displaying all the ruthlessness of their species. This may, however, bring about their downfall; by the time they've altered it to their satisfaction, the nest may be so weakened that it collapses, sparrows and all.

Sometimes a bird appears to get a bee in its bonnet and continues to pile up nest material long after it has collected enough for the job. A house sparrow once spent two weeks adding straw and yet more straw till its nest looked more like a straw sausage than anything else, stretched along the guttering of a garage. The whole process of breeding is a series of stereotyped activities, from the establishment of territory and the ritual of courting to nest-building, egg-laying and so on. Proceeding from one activity to the next requires the correct hormonal stimulus. If the stimulus is lacking, then the bird just carries on with the activity in which it is engaged, such as collecting nest material, until the chemistry hiccups it on to the next step or until it gives up, to try again next year.

Eggs

Birds' eggs come in all shapes, sizes and colours.

Cirl buntings' eggs are scrawled.

Dunnocks' eggs are an eye-catching invitation to the passing predator— why are they so strikingly coloured?

A ringed plover's clutch of eggs is practically indistinguishable from the surrounding pebbles.

Kingfishers lay the typically round white egg of birds which nest in dark holes.

Guillemots' eggs are pear-shaped. They spin easily and are thus less likely to roll off the nest-ledge.

Herring gulls lay the typical oval egg, with a large end tapering to a small one. The shape is well suited to occupy minimum space when there is a clutch of four. They are well camouflaged, so that the eggs have some protection if they are left unattended for a while.

The cuckoo's egg is adapted in both size and colour to make a close match with those of its predestined foster species.

Just as the smartest plumage wins the most desirable female, so the master cock bird knows the best feeding areas and the best nest positions. Clearly there is survival value in knowing your patch and ringing records show that individual birds return to the same place year after year. One numbered hen blackbird reared six broods from the same nest over a period of three seasons, though there were other suitable sites available. This particular nest was well supported by branches at the base and at the sides and it was located in a sheltered walled garden. With a certain amount of routine maintenance on the mud lining, the nest itself survived intact through the two winters involved. It was way back in 1740, long before anyone thought of numbered metal rings for birds' legs, that Johann Leonhard Frisch, a Berliner, tied red wool round the legs of swallows nesting near his house. His 'ringed' swallows returned to the same site year after year.

In those days, swallows were much addicted to building in disused chimneys. Indeed, they were called 'chimney swallows' until comparatively recently. They still use the occasional hollow tree but an outhouse or barn suits them better and they like to build their mud cups on a joist and up against something like a rafter. House martins

Above: Swifts pefer to collect their nest material in flight.

Right, above: House martins plaster their mud cups under the eaves. Note the different shades in the courses; at building time the mud is collected from different sources on different days.

Right, below: The kittiwake's nest is plastered to the sheer face of a cliff.

prefer to stay outdoors; their nests are plastered against a wall but protected from the rain by an overhanging eave, which forms a lid. They collect their building mud from two different sources and the whole structure is built to a well-defined architectural plan. The baseline is first plastered to the wall and forms the very bottom of the cup. Bringing one mud-gobbet at a time, the birds lay courses which are four beakfuls wide at the base tapering to two beakfuls wide at the lip of the cup. They collect mud from the two different sources on alternate days and, if the two muds dry to different colours, each day's work is clearly defined. The birds lay several courses a day, exactly as a human bricklayer lays bricks or concrete blocks.

There is another construction-site parallel in the technique they use. As Gilbert White noted many years ago, each pellet of mud is worked into its position with a vibrating movement of the head. Today's building contractors, laying concrete foundations and using bulk ready-mix, insert a vibrating rod into the wet mass of concrete to encourage it to mix and settle well into its place. The mud gobbets represent the martin's bricks. It is recorded that 2,575 were used to build one nest, which was twelve days in the making. The reason for using two mud sources is not clear but presumably the subtle differences in character bestow some cohesive advantage on the nest.

Swallows and martins are birds of the air, reluctant to come to the ground and obviously ill-at-ease there. With short legs designed to tuck away and reduce airflow, they are forced to shuffle about awkwardly to pick up mud. Swifts do not even deign to come to earth to collect nest material. Instead, they collect straw and feathers from the wind itself, then stick them to their nest site with saliva. Doubtless, they would opt out of earth-bound nests altogether, if they could find a way of supporting their eggs in the sky. Much the same is true of the ocean-going seabirds, which come only reluctantly to the most remote cliffs and islands to breed, since they cannot incubate an egg on the rolling waves. Like swifts, kittiwakes have such short legs that they hardly walk a step; they plaster their nests in house-martin fashion against the sheer faces of a cliff. The heavily-built and solid-boned divers only come ashore to breed, and, at a great disadvantage, nest only a few short waddles from the water's edge.

Only the legendary and mythical Halcyon broods its eggs at sea. Alcyone, daughter of Aeolus, was wife to Ceyx. In a storm at sea, Ceyx

Herring gull's nest, with an untypical clutch of eggs of three different colours.

was washed overboard. Alcyone threw herself after him in her grief. The gods took pity and changed them both into kingfishers (halcyons). Even now, we call a glassy windless calm in high summer a halcyon day, a day of stillness, while the kingfisher broods its eggs in a nest floating to eternity.

Once the nest of the more prosaically land-based bird is finished, only one formality stands between the mated pair and the delivery of the eggs which will furnish that nest. The timing of copulation is as carefully adjusted as are all the other pieces in the breeding jigsaw, so that the future family will derive greatest advantage. Courtship achieves its natural climax so that the small birds' eggs are laid in time for the resulting nestlings to benefit from the peak caterpillar populations of May and June. Sparrowhawks delay their nuptials a little, so that their chicks will arrive when the songbird chicks are already fattening nicely! Pigeons can and do breed freely almost through the year but only because they are

able to feed their new born young on 'milk' secreted from the lining of the crop, allowing them to translate the hard seeds they will have been feeding on into a substance fit for the delicate stomach of a chick.

The sex organs of birds are inactive most of the year and reduced in size, thus helping to reduce the all-up flying weight, but in the run-up to the breeding season the female ovaries and the male testes enlarge dramatically. Some of the hen's ova ripen, accumulate yolk sacs and proceed down the oviduct. The act of copulation is preceded by displays which, according to the species involved, may be anything from decidedly elaborate to downright perfunctory. In due course, the female crouches low and lifts her tail in an inviting posture. The cock bird mounts her, gripping a bunch of feathers at her neck with his bill, and their ventral openings meet in coitus. With a muscular spasm, the male presents a charge of sperm-filled seminal fluid to the oviduct of the female. Only in the case of waterfowl do the males have penises, because they often copulate under-water, when there might be a danger of fertilizing the water instead of the duck.

Eggs are all egg-shaped, of course, but there is a

certain amount of variation between different species. Some are oval, some elliptical and some almost spherical. They may be blunt-nosed, broad in the beam, short or long. Typically, they are oval, like the domestic hen's, with a larger end tapering to a narrower one. The shape is convenient for rolling and turning, so that warmth is distributed evenly, and the egg is relatively comfortable for sitting on. Eggs are extraordinarily strong. I vividly remember being invited to stand my twelve stone carefully on top of an eight inch long egg at an ostrich farm in South Africa and the nonchalant air of the farmer who knew that there was no danger at all that the egg would collapse. (Since the egg was already destined for an artificial incubator, I did not need to consider the parents' feelings!)

The eggs of guillemots and, to a lesser extent, razorbills are pear-shaped, though they lack the pronounced waist of the fruit. These auks habitually lay them on precipitous cliff ledges, where they roll round in circles rather than toppling off the narrow ledges. They are strikingly and individually patterned so that the birds can recognize their own egg. This is important as the birds do not make any sort of nest and the eggs may get shuffled about during the incubation period.

Typically, species which nest in dark holes, such as woodpeckers and owls, lay white eggs (as do reptiles). Other eggs come in a delightful range of colours, produced by two pigments, one of which is basically blue and green and the other basically brown, red and black. The eggs may be marked with fantastic specklings, scribblings and blotches, which provide a measure of camouflage to those laid in exposed nests, where they will be at risk when the brooding bird leaves them for any reason, but it is not easy to account for the survival values displayed by some strikingly coloured eggs. Inevitably, birds must, on occasions, leave the nest for a few minutes, during which time the eggs are perfectly safe in terms of incubation heat, but where is the sense to a songbird in leaving a cupful of brightly-coloured eggs to catch the magpie's eye? Compare, say, the dunnock's eye-catching clutch with that of a ringed plover or a little tern, whose eggs are well-nigh invisible a yard from your nose.

The number of eggs in a clutch varies from species to species. Also, some birds will continue to lay if for some reason they have lost eggs. Thus, if you persistently take a herring gull's eggs, it will lay more, striving to complete its 'norm' of three or four eggs. The domestic hen, producing almost an egg a day for several years, is perhaps the best example of this generous behaviour. Other birds, such as the pigeon, invariably lay a clutch of two eggs and no more, although in most fixed-clutch species there is a degree of tolerance, plus or minus an egg. Even if an egg is lost by some mischance, these birds will only lay their fixed number. It is useful to know the clutch size for a particular species in order to judge whether egg laying is still in progress or whether perhaps the nest has been robbed. Also, on occasion, two females may patronize the same nest; the result is an extravagant number of eggs. The average clutch for a blue tit is eleven but there is a record of nineteen in one nest, so it may be difficult to decide how many birds are responsible!

I knew of a pair of robins, which nested on a garage shelf, laying two eggs and then abandoning the nest. A week later they built another nest two feet away on the same shelf and laid a small clutch of four eggs which they reared successfully. They then went back to the first nest, complete with its two dead eggs, laid another four in it and successfully reared this brood as well. They then returned to nest number two, laid four more eggs and sat on them. They produced fourteen eggs in all, twelve of which hatched. Not surprisingly, this pair began nesting in February and they were supported by generous hand-outs of cheese.

Clutch sizes vary according to geographical latitude; birds belonging to the same species tend to lay more the further north they are nesting. In this way they are able to benefit from the longer foraging days but, since the northern season of plenty is shorter, there will be less chance of additional broods.

Some tits commonly lay a dozen eggs but seabirds tend to lay very few. Two eggs or even one is a typical number. This reflects their fortunate lot in terms of life expectancy. A small bird is lucky to reach maturity and, if it does so, it must produce a quantity of hopeful progeny. Seabirds may be several years in growing sexually mature but, paradoxically, are more likely to reach that happy state than smaller birds. They have, therefore, less need for quantity production. Guillemots lay one egg only. One of the benefits of their noisy, cliff-ledge society is that they are able to synchronize the activity. The colony lays its eggs more-or-less on the same day and the birds share the benefits of common interest in terms of 'togetherness' and a united front against predators.

5
Family Life

Guillemots breed sociably on remote sea cliffs.

Most birds sit tight as soon as they have produced the required number of eggs, for the sight of the full clutch stimulates an urge to brood. Some birds of prey and herons, however, begin to sit as soon as the first egg is laid, so that the hatching dates of the brood are staggered, for reasons which will become apparent. For all sitting birds, it is a time which involves great risk. Camouflage plumage is put to the test, for predators like weasels and magpies have a strong interest in the eggs, not to speak of the bird itself.

Sometimes both birds of the pair take turns at brooding, in which case both will have cryptic coloration. If the birds are sexually dimorphic, with significantly different plumages (for example, bright males and dowdy females), then that is an indication that the female will do the job. In order to develop, the embryonic chick needs continuous warmth; this is provided by the brood spot, a bare patch on the parent's underside revealed by the timely moulting of an area of down feathers. A healthy supply of blood vessels near the skin surface radiates heat, which reaches the eggs when the brooding bird wriggles and settles herself onto them, tucking them warmly against the soft and insulated nest lining. The average incubation temperature reaches 34°C. If the males share in incubation, they too have brood patches. Ducks do not have brood patches at all but provide exceptionally well-lined nests. Seabirds like gannets and cormorants have no brood patches, either, but they make up for it by having feet which are liberally supplied with blood vessels; they transfer heat to the egg when they stand on it carefully before settling.

Long incubation periods, some even lasting the best part of two months, are characteristic of species which are single-brooded or nest in secure positions relatively safe from predators; shorter periods of about a fortnight, or as little as eleven days in the case of some warblers, are usual for birds which are at risk in open nests. These differences are also reflected in the actual size of the egg. Larger ones are typical of 'precocial' birds, whose chicks take longer to incubate and are more highly developed on hatching; smaller ones

Whimbrel at typical nest site. The pair will share incubation for about twenty-four days. The young, being well developed at birth, will soon leave the dangers of the nest area.

are typical of 'altricial' birds, whose chicks result from a short incubation which leaves them naked, blind and helpless at birth.

During incubation, the growing embryo absorbs the white and most of the yolk from its egg. Towards the end of its time, it absorbs lime from the egg shell, thus strengthening its bones at the same time as it weakens the shell, making it easier to break free. It is, of course, able to breathe freely, as the egg shell is porous. As it nears the end of its term, the embryo moves about and flexes its muscles. At this time, the adult bird will deliberately touch the egg with its bill, calling quietly in answer to the embryo's cheep. A couple of days before hatching, the chick is sensitive to sounds. By learning language and recognizing the voice of its parents, the chick is finding its own identity and establishing a close relationship with the parents; in turn, it becomes imprinted on them as an individual.

For the taxing operation of breakthrough, the chick typically rests on its back or side. The horny pip which has developed on the tip of its upper mandible is presented to the upper surface of the shell. This 'egg tooth' is used as a knife, cutting into the egg shell as the chick taps steadily with its head describing an arc. If all goes well, a clean-cut escape-hatch is made. After it has done its job, the egg-tooth soon drops off. Emergence from the egg may take only a couple of minutes for a songbird or as much as a couple of days for a swan. The exhausted nestling emerges, to be welcomed by its parents and to settle down to a period of comfort and brooding while it dries. As soon as it is convenient, the parent will dispose of the tell-tale pieces of egg shell, although birds of prey may not bother since they have less to fear from unwelcome visitors. In the case of ground-nesting birds like partridges and lapwings, the chicks leave the nest very soon after hatching, so the parents are less likely to bother with the shells. These precocial chicks are already well developed by the time they are hatched, with eyes open and a fair amount of downy plumage. They very soon begin to feed for themselves and they are safer on the move. In contrast, songbird nestlings, which are the product of smaller eggs and short incubation, will emerge from the broken shell blind, naked and helpless. These altricial species are therefore even more dependent on their parents, since they will be

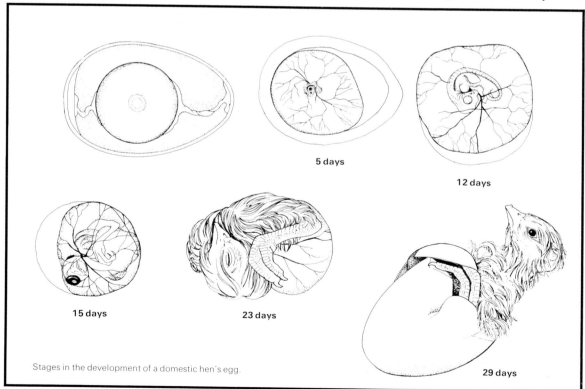

5 days

12 days

15 days

23 days

29 days

Stages in the development of a domestic hen's egg.

Above: Blackbird with young chicks. They are fed by both parents and will not leave the relative safety of the nest till they are two weeks old.

Right: A young turtle dove being fed by regurgitation. For its first few days the parent produces a form of milk from its crop lining, but this is soon supplemented with choice soft food or seeds.

When its eggs or chicks are threatened the lapwing attracts attention away from the nest with a distraction display, feigning injury.

The hen pheasant is well camouflaged, but the open ground nest is vulnerable to predators. Very soon after hatching the hen leads the chicks away to a life on the move.

confined to the nest for a further period before they venture out. Their mouths have brightly coloured gapes, designed to persuade the parents to fill them with food immediately!

The sex ratio among the nestlings is not quite random. Though you will hear talk of a 'pigeon pair', the only truth is that pigeons invariably lay two eggs. Quite apart from anything else, it is very difficult indeed to sex young pigeons; it is necessary to wait till they are almost fully grown before the fuller head and deeper keel of the more thickset cock reveals itself. Even then, there are large hens and small cocks to confuse the issue. Pigeons are unusual in that they feed their young on pigeon milk, a curd-like secretion which they produce in their crops. Presumably, they are only able to produce enough to nourish two squabs. Perhaps the 'pigeon pair' tradition is a not-too-subtle hint of the desirability of having only two

children because of the expense. For birds which are the classic symbol of love and fertility, this seems a bit hard.

There is some evidence that, in a mated pair of birds, the more perfectly plumaged partner is likely to find his or her sex reproduced in their progeny. In experimental conditions, an American scientist found that particularly 'good-looking' male zebra finches mated with poorly plumaged females resulted in more sons than daughters and that the converse resulted in more daughters. It is not yet clear whether the union actually produced this biased sex ratio or whether the parents themselves decided it by ejecting unattractive progeny from the nest. Either way, the end result, in selection terms, was to favour the more attractive individuals.

Newly hatched nestlings are dependent on their parents, though the period of dependence will vary

greatly in duration according to the species. Ground-nesters and waterfowl leave the nest within days, while some cliff-nesting seabirds stay there for up to two months. The parents' responsibility is to keep the newborn nestling warm and to feed it, while continuing to protect it from predators and the weather. The soft, downy feathers of the very young chicks provide little protection, and in rain the parent bird will spread its wings to make sure the drops fall clear of the youngster till such time as its feathers have grown and been dressed with a coating of grease. Apart from cold winds and excess sunshine, parents will also have to beware of enemies like hawks, foxes and weasels. Weasels, especially, are excellent climbers, able to shin up a tree and explore the interior of a likely hole or a nest box. They may also tackle ground nesters like partridges or plovers, which is one of the reasons why these

birds leave the nest so promptly once they have hatched.

If lapwings or golden plovers are unlucky enough to come to close quarters with a predator, whether it be man or fox, the adult bird is torn between a desire to run and a desire to protect its young. In the event, it employs a 'distraction display' designed to resolve an intolerable situation. It feigns injury, calling plaintively in order to be sure of attracting attention, hobbling over the ground with 'broken' legs and dragging a 'damaged' wing, only to take off and fly away when the intruder has been enticed a safe distance from the danger zone of the nest. All this time the chicks crouch, still and silent, till the parent returns by a circuitous route.

The lapwing chicks are early feeders, following close to their parents and copying their technique. The nestlings of garden songbirds, naked and helpless in their nurseries, rely totally on their parents. Their behaviour is at first entirely controlled by innate reactions to internal and external stimuli but time and experience give them a degree of reasoning. They are able to acquire learning, though at first sight they show little sign of it. As they become hungry, chemical triggers cause them to utter high-pitched peeping noises. Arrival of the parent, or almost anything else for that matter, evokes the gaping response, when the hairless, pink body reaches up a head with wide-open mouth. Seeing the bright colours inside the huge gape, the parent responds with food. The most insistent nestling gets the worm. He was probably the hungriest anyway but it makes sense that the strongest gets fed. Better for one to survive, if food is short, than that the whole brood is half-fed and starves. When the supplicant is full of food, he closes the gape, relaxes and falls back into the nest, silent again until the next hunger pangs, allowing a brother or sister a chance.

At this time, in early summer, there will be a great deal less of the territorial singing and mock battling that characterized spring. Quite simply, the birds are too busy. A pair of blue tits may be bringing an average of 700 caterpillars a day to the nest; an astonishing quantity. They have little time for the niceties of song and dance. Having adjusted their breeding cycle so that the hatchlings are emerging from their eggs just as the caterpillars are emerging from theirs, the parents take full advantage. They will take a tithe of the insects and larvae that are available, however the victims may hide, under leaves, in the soil, under tree bark.

Left: Young blue tits spend their first nineteen days in the safety of a hole nest. They are born at a time when caterpillars are abundant.

Below: Inside the nest cavity, the chicks respond with enthusiasm to the arrival of a parent. Seeing the bright colours inside the gape, the parent stuffs the chick with food till it relaxes and falls back to allow one of its siblings a chance. These nestlings are eight days old.

Right: The juvenile robin flutters its wings to beg for food. By the time it is five weeks old it will be independent.

under water or under a stone. Even the specialized seed-eaters like finches will be harvesting insects, for the very good reason that their young are unable to digest hard seeds, which are in any case in short supply at this time of year. Betraying their recent arrival in evolutionary terms, the young chaffinches and goldfinches will be fed on a variety of soft-bodied insect food.

The parent birds must choose food from whatever is available to present to their young. They will usually eat any small caterpillars to satisfy their own appetites, taking the larger ones back to the nest, thus making most efficient use of their time. If they have a large brood of nestlings, they may deny themselves and suffer accordingly. Perhaps another of the factors that militates against overlarge broods is that, being inclined to extra noisiness and cheeping, they are more likely to attract predators.

As the naked nestlings put on fat, so their contour feathers grow and provide protection and warmth. They need more food but the parents are allowed more time away from the nest to find it. Young blackbirds leave the safety of the nest when they are nearly two weeks old. They have a strong inborn tendency to follow their parents as soon as they become active. As fledglings, with their first flying suit of feathers, they flutter about uncertainly, highly vulnerable to predators and to 'rescue' by well-meaning but ill-advised people. The parents are never far away and, when danger threatens, they make a special 'chook' call, which warns the young to sit tight and play it cool. Do not feel impelled to gather up the 'lost' birds you

find in the garden borders, even when they tremble their wings and reach up to you with hungry gapes, asking to be fed. Quite apart from the fact that they are rarely abandoned, the task of caring for them is daunting. They need almost uninterrupted feeding through the hours of daylight. The task of returning them to the wild is also time-consuming and often fails. The best reason for not taking on the responsibility is that it is not necessary. Soon enough, the juveniles learn to make themselves scarce when trouble looms. Then, when the coast is clear, they utter a low chirping note which sends an urgent message of need and location to the parents. Both parents share the task of feeding the young and this grounded phase of family life lasts some three weeks.

As the days go by, the young birds learn to feed themselves by watching their parents. Their early efforts are clumsy, hit and miss affairs, with small reward, but they must acquire skills or perish. Turning, searching and pecking amongst leaves, discovering the bird table, being shown suitable food by the parents, the young will still display and beg, demanding food even though they are standing in an ocean of it, but soon enough they will imitate the parents with a hesitant stab, picking up a morsel, dropping it, picking it up again, till suddenly the penny drops. In time they will learn to listen for the clanging of the snail on a song-thrush's anvil and arrive in time to steal the fat mollusc from the unfortunate thrush.

Be warned that young birds in their first plumage may not look in the least the way you feel they should! Young sparrows look like young

sparrows but young robins do not look a bit like robin redbreasts. They are brown, spotty and leggy, though they have the right kind of plump shape and jaunty air. By their first winter, they have moulted to adult plumage and from then on you will have difficulty in telling cock from hen, let alone this year's robin from last year's.

Developing robins and thrushes are fed at ground level, tits and finches in the trees but young swallows are fed in the air, having gone solo after about three weeks on the rooftops. The beak-to-beak transfer of insects in the air is a thrilling process to watch; the parent hovers with great skill as it feeds the young on the wing. The swallow is characteristically a master pilot, skilled in aerobatics, swerving, banking and jinking with perfect control. The bird is completely at home in its aerial territory.

Not all young birds are fed on worms and caterpillars, by any means. Waterfowl soon learn to crop grass. Gulls and herons peck at their parents' beaks, causing them to sick up a cropfull of warm, half-digested fish: the perfect meal. Raptors bring whole but dead rabbits, voles and small birds for their young, tearing off strips of raw meat and offering them with tender solicitude. The young soon learn to claw and tear for themselves with their strongly hooked bills.

Above: By the time they are a week old, shelducklings are becoming independent as the brood tie weakens. They will join with another brood as readily as return to their mother in response to an alarm.

Right, above: Like many shelducks, puffins are born in an underground burrow. But they stay below for six weeks or so, fed on a diet of sand eels, brought back in bulk after the parent's fishing trips.

Right, below: The avocet has wandered too close to a shelduck family and is being warned off by an aggressive female.

Kestrels and sparrowhawks hatch their young late in May, when the vole and small bird population is ripe for harvesting. The fat furry vole is the prime food source for kestrels but, if voles are hard to come by, the hunting male will hover for small birds, such as a young lapwing or a skylark. Falcons or hawks, the young get painstaking attention. Fresh-killed prey is brought to the female at the nest. The female tears strips of flesh and offers them to the nestlings in turn. Their growth rate is rapid and their demand for food increases day by day. The adults need two voles a day to sustain themselves; the young need one

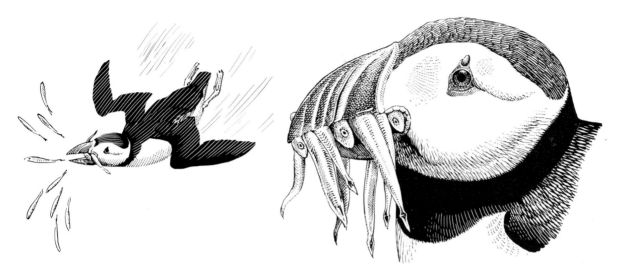

vole, increasing to two, to maintain a healthy start. To feed himself and his whole family, therefore, the male kestrel must catch a dozen voles or half a dozen young starlings each day. Working from seven in the morning to eight at night, he must catch a vole an hour. This is not difficult in fine weather and a good vole year. By the time they are three weeks old, the juveniles can feed themselves from food provided by the parents. Not until August, when they are strong on the wing and fully aerobatic, are they able to fend for themselves.

While the birds of prey are solicitous of their young, some of the waterfowl seem almost careless, to the superficial glance. Mallards have a decidedly permissive approach to the whole business of breeding and chick losses are prodigious. Shelducks, too, lose their new-hatched ducklings at an alarming rate, to crows and gulls as well as to terrestrial mammals which prey on them as they make the hazardous journey from their rabbit-burrow nests to the muddy feeding grounds of the estuary. By the time they are twenty-four hours old, the ducklings may have made a forced march of anything up to four miles across fields and ditches. By the time they are a week old, the family bond is already weakening.

This golden eagle will take its prey back to the eyrie where it will tear strips off the rabbit and offer them with tender solicitude to the eaglets.

As the brood-tie loses its grip, the ducklings join with members of the nearest brood in times of alarm as easily as they will flock to their own mother. Soon the intermingling of broods is so complete that there may be as many as a 100 ducklings gathered together in a 'crèche', with only one pair of adult birds to be seen.

The absent adults are not as uncaring as it may seem. They have endured a testing time during

black-backed gulls or by crows, individuals are less likely to be selected so long as the predators are confused by the bunching together of the alarmed group.

Like the young shelducks by an estuary, young puffins are born underground in a rabbit burrow, by the sea coast, and there they stay safely underground for nearly six weeks while they fatten up on sand eels. These are nutritious but rather small and it would be hopelessly inefficient for the adult to struggle all the way from the feeding grounds to the cliff slopes with one at a time. The little fish are abundant in inshore waters in June, when the eggs hatch, and the puffin dives in pursuit of them, flashing through the water, propelled by its narrow paddle-wings. In the sand-eel shoal, it snaps its head to left and right, collecting and storing the fish in its mouth. Both the tongue and the upper mandible are serrated, so that the fish are firmly gripped by their heads, with their tails hanging outside the beak. As each fish is caught, it is forced well back onto the tongue, which progressively reaches up to secure them against a groove in the roof of the mouth. Though it is often said that the fish are symmetrically arranged, with the heads and tails sticking out alternately, this is not so. The tails hang out on either side according to the random way in which they were caught. The important thing is that inside the mouth there is a row of heads neatly lined up fore and aft, firmly held in place by the tongue pressing upwards against the mandible. The sand-eels are carried back like this, a dozen or so at a time, to the young bird waiting in its underground burrow. There comes a time when the parents desert the young one, which fasts for a few days before emerging at night to make its own way to the sea to learn to fish for itself.

Guillemots, closely related to the puffins, also feed their young on small fish like sand eels but they regurgitate a warm mess of fish straight into the chick's mouth. Lined up on the death-defying ledges of sheer cliffs, the young guillemots live cheek-by-jowl with hundreds of their peers. They cannot walk more than a pace without bumping into a neighbour or falling off the edge, so they stand still and grow. Since the colony acts almost as an individual, the eggs were laid and in due course hatched synchronously. The young all achieve the age of three weeks on the same day, when they are firmly encouraged by their parents to launch themselves off the cliff face and more-or-less to plummet to the sea below. There the female

incubation, when they may lose a great deal of weight by metabolism of their body fat. When the crèche system relieves them of the responsibility of caring for their young, they are released to feed, to restore lost body tissue and to fatten themselves in preparation for the moult-migration flight which they must undertake before the ducklings are full-grown. From the point of view of the ducklings, there is safety in numbers. Attacked by great

Probably most birds mate for life, given the chance. Swans certainly maintain stable relationships. This pair is rearing six cygnets at Marazion marsh, in west Cornwall, with the castle on St Michael's Mount in the background.

Terns do not breed until their fourth year. Here a sandwich tern offers a choice morsel to its young.

will abandon the chick to its father, who feeds it, in the process teaching his offspring to fish. Father and chick stay together for a few months, mostly paddling about on the sea and rarely flying unless they are disturbed. They are often to be seen swimming together, the juvenile in the shadow of the adult male, always close by, near the south Devon coast in the late autumn. Any chicks which stayed behind on the ledge at the time of the general exodus would very soon be picked off by gulls or crows on the lookout for an easy meal.

Apart from some of the truly pelagic seabirds, which attempt only one brood in the season, most birds will start again and lay a second clutch if the first fails to hatch for some reason or if the eggs or chicks are lost to predators. Even birds which are normally single-brooded are able to produce a replacement, especially if their loss occurs near the start of the breeding cycle, but they will inevitably have missed their timing for the peak food supply and it is axiomatic that the best-fed chicks are those most likely to survive the testing time of winter.

Many species regularly raise two, sometimes even three families with success, though this could take house martins, for instance, well into October or even November and it must be unlikely that the later young are able to put on enough fat to sustain their migrations. There is a record of a pair of our resident blackbirds rearing five families in one season, producing at least fifteen, probably sixteen young. No wonder juvenile mortality is so high among birds! If they all survived to breed, the

world would soon be covered in a carpet of blackbirds.

Most young birds part company with their parents at the time of the autumn moult. Some stay in the family through their first winter, till the territorial urge begins to reassert itself. Others, like the swans and geese, may retain a strong family tie through several seasons. The majority of birds, certainly all small ones, are capable of breeding in their first year, in the season after they were hatched. Some birds of prey, including owls, and geese wait till their second year. Storm petrels breed in their third year. Terns, most gulls and gannets breed in their fourth year. The adolescent fulmar remains at sea for the first three or four years of its life and may not breed until it is seven years old, an age unattainable for the vast majority of passerines.

The guiding principle in the matter of bird populations is that breeding territories maintain the same number of breeding pairs. Since the supply of food is the main factor, a bird without a breeding territory simply does not breed. As a result, the food supply exerts a running check on numbers.

Most birds sit tight on their clutch of eggs when it is complete, so that the embryos hatch at very short intervals. They all have a more-or-less equal chance to survive. The procedure is very different in the case of some birds of prey and herons. They start to incubate as soon as the first egg is laid, continuing to lay the rest of the clutch at two-or-more-day intervals. The result is that the hatch is

Barn owls, like some other birds of prey and herons, start to incubate as soon as they lay the first egg. The result is a brood of owlets with an age-range of sizes. The eldest has an advantage at feeding time and is more likely to survive.

staggered. A nest of owlets will show a significant range of sizes from eldest to youngest. The two-day start that the eldest has on his siblings gives him a real advantage and he does not hesitate to use it. If there is a shortage of food, the youngest invariably succumbs; if there is an unusually large brood, the youngest probably dies anyway and may well be eaten by one of its brothers or sisters. While the number of breeding pairs remains more or less constant, the success of the family depends on the abundance or otherwise of the prey. Even the size of the owl clutch may be adjusted according to food availability. In a good mouse year, the parents will try extra eggs; in a bad year, fewer. If hunting becomes difficult, the male may be unable to find enough to sustain the female, who has to abandon the nest. In a catastrophic year, they may not even attempt to nest at all.

Probably, most birds mate for life, given the chance, but small birds do not live long, so it is the larger ones, like swans, which get the reputation for fidelity in marriage. The advantages of life partnership are real. If you already know your mate, then the annual courtship formalities may be shortened, leaving more time and energy for the practical side of breeding. But it is not easy to be dogmatic about the long-term effectiveness of the pair bond, since in spring the birds may be returning not so much to a known partner as to a known nest site, where last year's mate is conveniently to hand. Certainly, there is the bird equivalent of divorce as a result of incompatibility and, if one partner dies, the other will look for a replacement. Common sense prevails. The survival advantages in a successful marriage ensure that the institution has an assured future.

There is a great deal of evidence in support of these assertions about marriage, especially from the waterfowl, which were easier to study as individuals in the days before numbered rings were invented. Marks on swan beaks revealed that the birds maintained stable relationships. In more recent studies at the Wildfowl Trust, it was found that the Bewick's swans, birds which regularly fly in for the winter, once paired, stay together for a number of years, some of them for at least eight and the longest for more than thirteen years. Out of the 1,300 known birds, there was no record at all of a pair parting company and then re-appearing with a new mate, except in cases where one partner was missing, presumed dead. In other words, there were no divorces. Widowed females very soon found new partners, as females are always much in demand. This is not to suggest that birds lead sober, blameless lives, with no hint of the darker sides of passion and philandery. Drake mallards on any park pond will demonstrate their zest for the chase, forcing themselves on unaccompanied females. Seizing their necks, they will hold the females underwater while they struggle to couple, sometimes even drowning the unfortunate duck in the process. Even when paired, the behaviour of mallard drakes leaves a lot to be desired. They hang about the nest site while the duck does all the work of incubation, then quietly slope off when the ducklings hatch and leave the mother to bring them up.

Polygamy is not unknown amongst birds. Cock wrens may serve more than one female. Cock robins may maintain two females, each of them jealously holding her own territory and barring it to the other. But the reverse situation, where the female has sexual relationships with more than one male, is rare indeed and almost invariably un-British. Possibly, it occurs when the males outnumber females in a population and is a formula which allows an emancipated female to devote more time and effort to feeding and maintaining herself in peak fitness, so that she may produce more clutches of eggs. As mentioned earlier, in the case of the red-necked phalarope it is the brightly plumaged female who takes the initiative in courtship, provides the dowdy male with the eggs for the nest which he has built and then leaves him to complete the task while she moves on to court another male. Possibly the dotterel is another example, for the incubation is undertaken mainly by the male bird. It has been suggested that the female cuckoo solicits more than one male but then it has been suggested equally that it is the male cuckoo which shops around!

The cuckoo is unique, in Britain, where it is the only parasitic bird. Cuckoos opt out of family life altogether by fostering their eggs the moment they are laid. In other parts of the world, other birds use the same methods, while, for that matter, in other parts of the world, not all cuckoo species are parasitic. In fact, most of them build nests in the conventional way but many are notoriously bad at nest-building and tend to lay eggs in an undisciplined way, at odd intervals and sometimes in someone else's nest. Cowbirds will steal another bird's nest but then incubate their own eggs in it. House sparrows will take over a house martin's nest by brute force, perhaps demonstrating one step along the road to parasitism.

Long ago, our cuckoos found that they could perpetuate their species by producing eggs which mimicked those of some small bird. The cuckoos then laid eggs in the nest of this bird, which became a 'host'. The system works well from the point of view of the cuckoo and not disastrously from the point of view of the host, since it is not in the interest of the parasitic cuckoo for its host species to die out. The cuckoo must not be *too* successful. Dunnocks have been prime targets for cuckoos for many years yet it is estimated that there are over three million of them nesting in Britain alone.

Since it does not go to the trouble of building a nest, the cuckoo has the luxury of a couple of extra

weeks of winter warmth in Africa and is by no means the first of our summer visitors. Once on our shores, it returns to the kind of country where it was hatched and stakes out a territory, calling 'cuckoo' to attract a mate. The reason it returns to the habitat of its birth is because it is 'fixed' on a particular host species and will only parasitize a victim belonging to the species of its own foster parents. We tend to speak of a 'rock pipit cuckoo' or a 'reed warbler cuckoo' or a 'dunnock cuckoo'. If the female was hatched in a reed warbler's nest, that is where she will lay her own eggs. She spies out the land and charts all the reed warbler activity. Timing is critical. The mated cuckoo waits and watches. When the reed warbler lays its first egg, she must remove it and replace it with her own, without causing the rightful owners of the nest to desert. The moment the warbler has left its single egg in the nest and flown off, the hen cuckoo flies in, picks up the warbler egg in her beak, turns to lay her own directly in its place and flies away, never to return. Her alien egg closely resembles the warbler's in both colour and size. Over the next few days, the host will complete her clutch in ignorance of the substitution. The cuckoo's egg even has the same incubation period as the warbler but, laid first, it will be likely to hatch first, giving an important advantage to the nestling cuckoo, who deals promptly with the opposition. He may be naked and blind but he has strong legs and wing stumps. Wriggling and manoeuvring, he heaves each of the warbler's eggs in turn onto his back,

In the foster-parent tree-pipit's nest, a newly hatched cuckoo ejects the opposition to become sole occupant. The parents will ignore their own eggs once they are outside the nest cup.

then pushes them out of the nest. If by chance he was not the first to hatch, he ejects the nestlings instead of the eggs. Once out of the nest, they will be totally ignored by the parents.

The gaping action of a hungry chick is a major stimulus to the returning foster parents. They feed it. The cuckoo needs all the food that his erstwhile nestmates would have received, because he is going to grow faster and bigger than they would have, and he has assured himself of the full-time attention of his adoptive parents. In human terms, the affair is callous and horrific but, for the new-born cuckoo, it is a simple question of survival. Either the reed-warbler's rightful chicks go or he goes. His natural mother, meanwhile, has been busy finding anything up to a dozen nests, always of the same species. If she is successful, in due course she will have found homes for a dozen eggs which will produce monster chicks with monster gapes to tax the host's hunting prowess. The fat cuckoos will be off to Africa at the end of summer, to return next spring to yet more reed warblers or dunnocks or whatever it is that they are pro-grammed to parasitize.

Although it never knew its mother's voice, the yearling cuckoo will sing 'cuckoo' simply because this comes naturally to it. The rudiments of language are genetically implanted, then refined by exposure to other singers in the first season but, as the bird was deprived of experience, the song, not surprisingly, is limited, and there is not much scope for polishing. The cuckoo's song lacks the sophisticated variations which are so character-istic of more conventional songbirds. Though they may start with nothing more than a song-sheet, complete with what musicians call 'the dots', songsters like thrushes and nightingales soon progress from a colourless sequence of notes to an imaginative and musical performance which improves with age.

Birdsong is mostly a daytime activity. At night, people feel, all self-respecting birds should be tucked up in bed asleep. In fact, birds sleep at odd times throughout the day and night. Whether they are active by day or by night is related to their feeding habits rather than their sleeping habits. In summer they will spend more time feeding than roosting, though if food is plentiful they may go earlier to bed. Wading birds, which feed when the tidal mudflats are uncovered, work to a tidal rhythm, feeding when the tide is out, whether it is day or night time.

During the breeding season, birds generally roost in their territories but, afterwards, it is typical of those which feed together that they roost together. The finches and starlings, which kept themselves to themselves, will now be gathering in multi-family groups to search for food, though chaffinches will part and all-male parties will forage together. It makes sense for them to sleep together as well. Sparrows, never very territorial at the best of times, search the country in loose-knit gangs. In late autumn, house martin families will still be going home to their nests at night, though when they have flown these same sanctuaries may serve for sparrow roosts. Swallows gather in enormous numbers on telephone wires but go to roost in places like reed-beds, where they funnel down at dusk to cling tight to the vertical stems. Hole nesters tend to roost in holes, most tits in

solitary splendour; starlings make a noisy exception. Tree creepers sleep alone, hollowing out an egg-shaped burrow in the soft bark of the Californian redwood and pressing themselves tightly in, beaks pointing to the sky and feathers well fluffed. Many birds find a hole or crevice in a tree trunk or an old building. Blue tits may find a way into a street lamp, where they have the added benefit of central heating. Pied wagtails, relatively unsociable in the breeding season, assemble after it and roost gregariously in great numbers, in city centre trees or in horticultural glasshouses, comfortably warm.

The main advantage of a communal roost is that in cuddling together the birds conserve energy. Wrens may carry that logic to excess, as mentioned earlier, cramming themselves into nestboxes in astonishing numbers. Severe winters hit them hard, so it makes sense for them to join together in beating the cold. Small birds like wrens have a lot of surface area in relation to their volume. Surface area directly affects heat loss. That is why, each day, they must eat a greater proportion of their body weight than larger birds. Humming birds do not even try to keep warm at night; they chill to a state of torpor.

I once watched as a steady stream of twenty wrens made their unobtrusive way into a tit box at dusk. One of my correspondents wrote of thirty-five descending on her nest box. Even that is nowhere near the record. There was a tit box in Norfolk, just $4\frac{1}{2} \times 5\frac{1}{2} \times 5\frac{3}{4}$ inches ($11\cdot4 \times 14 \times 14\cdot6$ cm), which served as a dormitory for no less than sixty-one wrens. Each bird occupied $2\frac{1}{3}$ cubic inches (38 cu. cm) of space. Apparently the last

arrivals were so desperate to get into the warm that they grouped themselves together and barged in the entrance hole like a rugby scrum. Only one of these birds died; presumably this was the effect of cramped quarters on a bird which was already in poor condition. It is not likely that suffocation was the cause of death; at night bird metabolism slows down and there is a reduced requirement for oxygen.

Birds which roost in the open go to a great deal of trouble to find shelter. Blackbirds will choose thick foliage on the lee side of a building if they have the choice. They also take a lot of trouble to keep warm. Provided they are well fed, they are able to manage this. Fluffing out their contour feathers increases the insulating layer of warm air against their skin, in the manner of a string vest. Their heads are turned so that the bill is tucked away among the feathers on the back, not, incidentally, under the wing. Pigeons prefer to lean forwards, hunching their heads but not tucking them back. Most passerines look headless and rounded when they rest.

Carrion crows enjoy reputations as solitary birds but in fact roost communally in quite large numbers outside the breeding season. That is true of all the crow family, including jays, magpies and ravens. There may be a hundred or so together; there may be thousands. They settle, call and circle again with noisy excitement before finally settling down for the night, high above the ground, in their chosen piece of woodland.

Swifts may roost on the wing, though at breeding time they will settle on the nest. Observation by radar has shown that they fly high

The female cuckoo takes a reed warbler's egg in her bill and lays her own egg directly into the nest. The cuckoo egg will resemble a reed warblers in both size and colouration.

Having eliminated all opposition, the fledgling cuckoo gets the undivided attention of its foster parent. It is usual for cuckoos to foster on wrens, presumably because of the juvenile's food requirements must be near the limit of the small foster-parent's capacity to collect.

Swallows gather together in large numbers at the end of the breeding season, to roost at night in places like reed-beds.

densities on a mighty scale. It seems that these displays help to locate the roost site and also act as a navigation mark to assist the incoming parties in making a correct landfall. High winds or rain cut short the performance but even in these conditions the incoming flocks mark the spot long enough to guide in the next squadron, then funnel down to roost, leaving the newcomers to take over the signalling. On a good night, the swooshing, rocketting and funnelling of massed swarms of starlings in these aerial displays is one of the most exciting natural events to be seen anywhere, at any time.

As the seemingly endless black stream funnels down, each individual flies in to land at its own bedside. Whether it is to grasp the stem of a reed or the twig of a sycamore or a ledge of the Bank of England, each has its own chosen perch. As in all small birds, a starling's hind toe is opposed to the others and the flexor tendons are so arranged that, when the bird relaxes, its grip tightens, a comfortable arrangement which ensures that the bird does not fall out of bed the moment it goes to sleep. Before it joins its neighbour in sleep, shoulder to shoulder for warmth, it sings with its fellows the evening chorus, a volume of sustained twittering which rises above the noise of city traffic.

The practice of using city-centre buildings as roost places is a relatively recent habit for starlings, dating back to the turn of the century. The first known location was Nelson's Column in Trafalgar Square, which is still well and truly operational. A well-established roost may, over a period of years, become home for anything up to 50,000 individuals. One of the prime requirements is shelter from wind and rain and the birds much approve of tall structures with an abundance of ledges and sills and the sort of ornamentation which produces eaves and cornices. A row of sculptured worthies sheltering in recessed niches serves well. Modern buildings of the slab-sided glass and concrete variety are despised by starlings, a judgement in which they are not alone.

If they get half a chance, starlings will choose sites which offer extra worth, such as ventilation outlets or industrial cooling towers. They derive a great deal of advantage from the so-called 'heat-island' effect which is characteristic of big cities. Large numbers of domestic and industrial fires, warm effluents, dust and smoke particles all encourage condensation of water vapour which creates an insulating layer of cloud, reducing heat-loss from the land into the atmosphere. In and

into the sky and settle into a rhythmic pattern in which they beat their wings for a few seconds, then rest for about the same time.

Though starlings are solitary birds during the early part of the breeding season, their family parties soon join together into those familiar raiding and swooping gangs which forage wherever food is to be found. It is no surprise that they gather for roosting in uncountable numbers. Towards sunset, the garden parties fly off to join with others. Following well-defined flight paths, perhaps covering as much as thirty miles, the groups coalesce into enormous flocks, a rush hour in reverse, with countless thousands making their purposeful way to the chosen rest-place. Reed-beds, rhododendron thickets, woods, shipyards, city centres all serve their purpose. The build-up begins in mid-June but reaches a peak much later in the year, after our home-bred birds are joined by a great influx of immigrants from the continent.

When the birds reach the vicinity of the roosting area, there will often be a spectacular flying display. Dense clouds of starlings fill the sky, sweeping back and forth, changing patterns and

Starlings are solitary birds during the early part of the breeding season, but later they join together in uncountable numbers at communal roosts.

around London there is a 7°C temperature difference between the urban and rural habitats, the built-up area being warmer. The difference is not so marked in smaller cities but is still significant. The effect is most apparent in a cold spell, when everyone stokes up the fire, using forty per cent more fuel than normal, to the greater benefit of the starling's comfort at night.

Thick mid-winter fog may bring disaster to roosting starlings. One record tells of 10,000 birds which were asphyxiated in smog while flying over the Mersey estuary on their way to roost. Other perils await the roosting birds. At a Warwickshire roost, the starlings were joined by three sparrow-hawks and a peregrine, which made uncomfortable bedfellows. Sparrowhawks have been seen making persistent attempts to strike down starlings as they were arriving to roost in a small conifer plantation in Galloway but their success rate was not great: of sixty attempts at chasing and striking, only two were positively successful. It is possible that the pre-roost evolutions of the swarming birds act as an effective anti-predator

device but they nevertheless do attract predators. Both peregrines and merlins were seen at the Galloway roost site.

The open air can be a dangerous place for birds. Peregrines will take many pigeons on the wing, screaming down at them in an eighty-mile-an-hour power dive. Even such aerial masters as swallows and swifts may fall victim to a peregrine or a hobby, whereas more low-level creatures like tits and finches are carried off by sparrowhawks. Tawny owls may leave their ivy-clad day roosts for a few seconds just to pick off a passing passerine; it is not surprising that if their hiding place is discovered they will be persistently bedevilled by the mobbing of small birds which draw the attention of all and sundry to the potential danger.

Most birds die within a couple of weeks of leaving the nest; it is their period of greatest danger, when they are taken by falcons, hawks, crows, weasels, cats, and both well- and ill-disposed small boys. In the unlikely event of a blackbird reaching eight weeks old, his chances are vastly improved and he has an expectation of eighteen months. Less than ten per cent of those leaving the nest will reach the age of five. Peak mortality is therefore in May and June. Apart from the predators so far mentioned, there are traffic accidents and garden and agricultural chemicals, to say nothing of everyday accident and injury. Birds frequently fly into windows, at best giving themselves a bruise, at worst killing themselves. The trouble often occurs when there are windows at each end of a room and the bird can see right through from the front to the back garden. It flies forward, full of confidence, only to be brought up with a jerk when it hits the glass. Venetian blinds may be the answer, or, perhaps, dirty windows! Anything to reveal to the bird the existence of the glass will help. On sunny days, the problem may be caused by a reflection of the garden, in which case blinds or curtains are no use. Outside netting solves the problem but is not very attractive. The cut-out shape of a sparrowhawk often works. One man who worked in a modern office block with a plethora of glass found that an average of six birds were being killed every week. He stuck up a buzzard silhouette with some success. Probably, any sort of pattern which breaks up the apparently inviting hole will do. The trouble occurs mainly in spring and summer, when birds are busy and fledglings learning to fly. It is not confined to diurnal birds; often enough, owls will fly into windows at night. If you find birds stunned under your window, the best treatment is to put them somewhere dark and very warm for an hour or so before quietly releasing them.

Other bird hazards are overhead wires. Avocets occasionally kill themselves on the heavy-duty electricity cables crossing the Tamar estuary, where they winter. Swans not infrequently collide with cables. Their rather poor forward vision means that they see the wires too late to manoeuvre their heavy bodies out of the way. Another hazard faced by swans is the increasing tendency of anglers to throw away large quantities of lead shot, which the swans subsequently ingest when grazing the bankside vegetation. Of 272 swans examined, it was found that ninety-two of them had lead pellets in their stomachs. Toxic chemicals and oil spills take a great toll of birds every year and so do the more natural effects of the weather.

Severe winters, with prolonged frost and snows, will make life difficult for birds by reducing the available food supply. In the fearful winter of 1962–3, the British wren population was reduced by a staggering three-quarters; song thrushes were reduced by a half. Herons and kingfishers, unable to get at their fish prey were also badly hit and it took some three or four years to re-establish their numbers. Birds are perfectly able to recover from natural disasters, which are part and parcel of the process of natural selection. It is the man-made disasters of habitat loss and pollution which cause long-term damage to populations.

On occasions, birds may redress the imbalance by passing some troubles back to us. Most bird maladies and diseases are not communicable to man but ornithosis (once called psittacosis) is a sort of virus pneumonia which birds like pigeons or gulls may transmit to us. It may be that we have to take more urgent steps to deal with the large numbers of town gulls, since the infection may be contracted through contact with their faeces. Gulls and cormorants also carry *Salmonella* and other bacteria; there is little evidence that these harm the birds but they create problems for us. Cormorants and gannets have been affected by outbreaks of Newcastle disease, a form of influenza, which can cause problems with domestic poultry but which also kills game birds and birds of prey.

The birds themselves are, of course, subject to attack by disease. Terns may suffer mass mortality when affected by an outbreak of 'flu. Puffinosis carried by gulls may result in many deaths to young shearwaters. Tuberculosis is the most commonly recorded disease of wild birds of prey and there are many other bacterial diseases to which they may fall victim. The chances of old age, one way or another, are remote.

Probably, most animals die unseen, for if they are sick or injured they tend to hide away in solitary misery. It is in the nature of things that, if they are in a weakened condition, either they recover quickly or something will come along to give them a quick end. In the wild, most lives are short. Life expectancy is measured in low figures, though potential life span may be surprisingly high. Broadly speaking, the larger the creature, the longer it will live; the longer it lives, the greater its expectancy will be. Its chances get better with every month survived. The exceptional goldcrest may reach the old age of three, a blackbird ten, owls and kestrels sixteen, a wild mute swan nineteen years.

Better to be a man, with an average expectancy of sixty-nine; even better to be a woman, who might make seventy-five, or an oak, which might make 500, or a yew, which could reach 1,000 years old. The moral is, if you want to live to a ripe old age, be a tree and plant yourself very, very carefully.

6
Movements and Migration

In winter, hard weather brings continental thrushes
like this fieldfare to search for berries.

When the breeding season is over, the bird world is one of movement and change, especially for those which feed mainly on insects and for those young birds which must leave the family and make their own way. Even in the case of a largely sedentary species like the heron, the young birds of the year must wander a little and fight to establish a feeding patch of their own. Birds in the south-east might just try their luck on the other side of the Channel. But there will be an equal and opposite exchange movement of French and Belgian birds hoping to find more sympathetic fishing in Britain.

The sedentary house sparrows spend their whole lives within a few hundred yards of the home they share with you and me but in autumn they will indulge in raiding parties to the nearest cornfields and a change of air. As the hard days of winter draw near, birds of the high mountain tops migrate down to the less demanding temperatures below.

As if life was not already hard enough in winter, the resident birds are joined by large numbers of foreigners which have migrated to us rather than away from us. Forsaking the barren tundra, vast numbers of wildfowl fly in to our estuaries and marshes. Fleeing the icy winter wastes of Scandinavia, fieldfares and redwings come in their thousands, to compete for the hawthorn and holly berries and for the rotting windfall fruit. In really bad weather, a well-stocked bird-feeding station will undoubtedly help many to survive. Home-bred blackbirds remain in Britain for the winter, although there is some movement from the north towards Ireland and southern England but their numbers are swelled by a considerable influx of continental birds which migrate across the Channel. Crossing at night, many lose their lives in collision with lighthouses. They are particularly vulnerable if they are caught in fog. Fishing vessels working offshore in a foggy dawn may well find that in a perfectly calm sea they are surrounded by drowned land birds. In these conditions, migrating birds frequently land on boats, or on anything else which gives them somewhere to rest.

Mistle thrushes form into flocks after the breeding season, feeding together in a more-or-less sociable way, keeping in loose contact by calling to each other as they forage for the berries of rowan and juniper. Those of the south tend to be sedentary, while those from northern parts of Britain join together in flocks and move south to winter; some even overshoot the land and visit France. Given a decent reserve of fat, they are well

Whooper swans breed in Iceland and Scandinavia, but fly south to winter in milder climates. They are fairly common visitors to the lakes and estuaries of northern Britain and Ireland.

able to stay warm; they even roost with snow on their plumage. The problem is to find enough to eat. Snails are hidden; so are the few insects which are left alive, deep in crevices or leaf litter. Foraging becomes a serious business; there is little time for singing or posturing. Only the fiercely territorial robin summons up enough energy to entertain us with a thin song. Hedges and gardens ring with the more workaday calls of finch and tit parties as they keep in touch with each other. The advantage of relatively short distance dispersals is that, as well as conveniently avoiding the cold, the birds discover different feeding prospects. In these local movements, there may lie a clue to the grander journeys of migration: for those birds which must eat insects, there is no option but to

travel long distances to warmer, insect-rich winters.

In years past, the concept of bird movements was much disputed. It seemed a more acceptable probability that insect-eaters slept through the winter, perhaps in a changed state connected with the moulting process, perhaps protected from the weather by crawling into the mud of a pond or perhaps just hidden away in a hollow tree or a rock crevice. In 1678, when Francis Willughby published his *Ornithology*, he summarized his thoughts about the cuckoo: 'What becomes of the cuckoo in the winter-time, whether hiding herself in hollow trees, or other holes and caverns, she lies torpid, and at the return of the spring revives again; or rather at the approach of winter, being impatient of cold, shifts place and departs into hot countrys, is not as yet to me certainly known. Aldrovandus writes, that it is by long observation found, that she doth in the winter enter into the hollows of trees, or the caverns of rocks and the earth, and there lie hid all that season. Some (saith he) tell a story of a certain country man of Zurich in Switzerland, who having laid a log on the fire in winter, heard a cuckoo cry in it. . . . But seeing it is most certain, that many sorts of birds do at certain seasons of the year shift places, and depart into other countrys, as for example quails, woodcocks, fieldfares, storks, etc. Why may not cuckoos also do the same? For my part I never yet met with any credible person that dared affirm, that himself had found or seen a cuckoo in winter-time taken out of a hollow tree, or any other lurking-place.'

It is clear that by the mid-seventeenth century people were well aware of the reality of migration. Of the swallow, Willughby wrote: 'What becomes of swallows in winter-time, whether they fly into other countries, or lie torpid in hollow trees, and the like places, neither are natural historians agreed, nor indeed can we certainly determine. To us it seems more probable that they fly away into hot countries, *viz. Egypt, Aethiopia*, etc than that they lurk in hollow trees, or holes of rocks and ancient buildings, or lie in water under the ice in northern countries as Olaus Magnus reports . . . I am assured of my knowledge (saith Peter Martyr) that swallows, kites, and other fowl fly over the sea out of Europe to Alexandria to winter.'

It was hard for people to credit that the frail little swallow could undertake two journeys of thousands of miles each year and though Gilbert White, a hundred years later, was virtually convinced that they did so, he allowed the faint possibility that they might 'conglobulate' in soft mud for the winter. It is easy to see how people could become misled, since swallows do indeed congregate in large numbers at the edges of muddy ponds, clinging to the tall stems of reeds at dusk to roost, only to have disappeared completely next morning when they finally decide to fly. The situation is further confused by the undoubted fact that some swallows do indeed spend the winter in the south-western part of England, just about surviving on a diet of grounded insects associated with rotting piles of seaweed on the beaches, and there are indeed birds which go into torpid states at times. At least one species, the American poorwill, goes into true hibernation, where else but in California.

It is important to be aware of late and early records for migratory birds, before jumping to the conclusion that you have discovered wintering individuals. House martins may well be breeding

Migration

The power of flight gives birds an enviable facility for world travel, searching out new pastures or enjoying an annual itinerary which takes advantage of widely separated seasons of plenty.

The British Isles. Blackbirds from the north migrate south to Ireland and southern England in winter.

Herons from the south-east swap with an equal and opposite movement of herons from northern France and Belgium.

Wildfowl from Siberia, Spitzbergen, Iceland and Scandinavia fly in to traditional feeding grounds like the Solway Firth, Severn Estuary or the Wexford Slobs for the winter.

Fieldfares migrate west from Scandinavia to winter in Britain in hard winters.

Ospreys pass through UK estuaries on passage from Scandinavia and Scotland on their way to south-west Spain and north-west Africa.

Sedge warblers breed in UK, migrate south to central and southern Africa for winter.

British swallows winter in the Johannesburg area.

Turnstones breed from Greenland to Siberia, winter in the UK, South Africa, South Australia and New Zealand.

Arctic terns breed in high arctic, 'winter' in the Antarctic summer, migrating by way of West Europe and the West African coast.

Barnacle geese - two separate populations. One breeds in South Greenland, winters on the coast in Northern Ireland. The other breeds in Spitzbergen, winters on the Solway Firth.

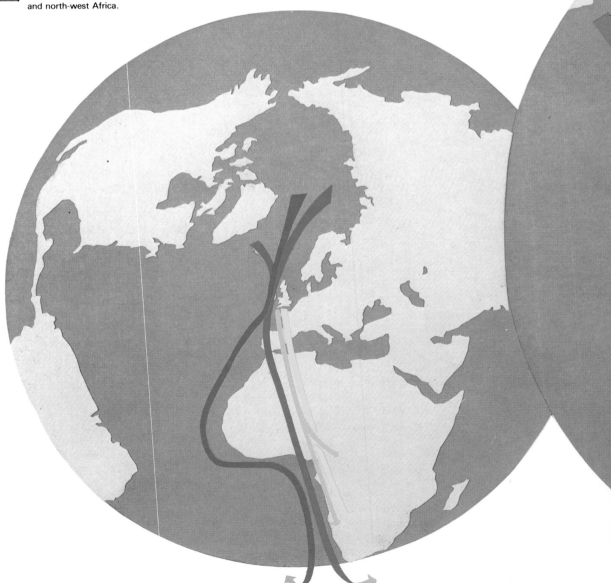

as late as November and even December before they finally leave the country. Early arrivals may show themselves in mid-February. Nevertheless, with the general amelioration of the climate which was typical of this century until recently, the extended growing season of autumn has encouraged a few summer visitors like chiff-chaffs and blackcaps to stay and enjoy milder winters with their increased insect food. However, for the overwhelming majority of our summer visitors, the shortening days and lowering temperatures of approaching winter signal the time to leave.

In the grand sense, migration represents an annual return ticket to far-away places, promising perpetual summer and plentiful supplies of food in return for successful completion of highly hazardous journeys. For the swallows, the signal to assemble into migratory flocks comes when the insect population falls below the point where it is providing adequate rations. Setting off from communal roosts at about the end of August into September, they start a 6,000-mile journey. Crossing the English Channel, they stream south across the western end of the Mediterranean. During October, they face a gruelling haul across 1,000 miles of the Sahara, where there is little chance of food or water, let alone rest. For most of their journey, they are able to travel in a leisurely fashion, stopping off at night, since they are able to refuel on the way. Because flying insects are available to them, swallows migrate almost at ground level, unlike most passerines.

Everyone knows about the swallows' journey,

Above: Black-tailed godwits nest in East Anglia and points east, but winter in the south west, and the western coasts of France and Spain.

Right: Like swallows, house martins breed almost everywhere in Britain, but migrate to spend the winter in South Africa.

mainly because we look forward with such pleasure to their return in spring. They are perhaps most people's idea of a migratory bird, but other birds cover greater distances by far. The turnstone makes prodigious journeys between his summer and winter quarters. Breeding in the arctic tundra of Greenland, east to Siberia, and taking advantage of the short but insect-rich summer, turnstones move south to winter anywhere from Britain by way of South Africa to South Australia and New Zealand. In May and September, we see a great influx on our shores and happily a fair number winter with us. Perhaps, one day, a pioneering pair of turnstones may take the plunge and breed in Britain.

The classic example of 'globe spanning' is that of the arctic tern. Many breed in Britain as summer visitors but these are at the extreme southern end of their range. More typically, they nest high up in the summer Arctic but then migrate from the very top of the world by way of Western Europe and the west African coast (others follow a different route down the western seaboard of America) to the deep Antarctic on the other side of the globe, a journey of some 11,000 miles. In other words they cover an incredible 22,000 miles a year to enjoy perpetual summer.

Those are the grand migration routes. Most of our familiar summer visitors fly a well-worn path no farther than southern France or Spain or across the Mediterranean to enjoy the tropical or sub-tropical warmth of Africa. They do not 'stock up' in anticipation of the journey so much as take advantage of the abundance of summer food, so that when times become less easy they have a reservoir of fuel to carry them to where life is good. A sedge warbler leaving our shores will lose half its body weight before it arrives in its African wintering quarters. A Greenland wheatear will fatten in July and August, to lose sixty per cent of his body weight in crossing half the north Atlantic to the west coast of Spain. A Scandinavian osprey will call at an English south coast estuary and spend two or three weeks enjoying the mullet and perhaps the odd salmon peal before continuing his passage to winter in Spain or Africa. Countless thousands of waders will call in at Morecambe Bay or the Wash on their passage south, in order to re-fuel on fat worms and shrimps and marine snails.

These migration movements involve aerial routes that criss-cross the whole of western Europe. Although the routes may come together at natural bottlenecks, like the Gibraltar crossing to Africa, the migrants are not following highways in the sky, as is sometimes suggested.

Back in Roman times, men attached woollen cords to pigeons which, carried far from home, nevertheless managed to find their way back again. That was not evidence of migration, of course, merely of a desire to return to sit on eggs but it showed a high degree of navigational ability. In the same way, swallows taken from Bremen in Germany and released in England returned home in four days. Manx shearwaters sent to Boston, USA, by air and released there flew 3,000 miles to their nest burrows on Skokholm island off Pembrokeshire in twelve and a half days.

We may have known for a long time that birds do such things but it is still by no means clear what navigational methods they use. In the simplest form of navigation, birds (or sailors) need only know compass direction and time required to cover the distance involved. There is no doubt that birds are able to determine an azimuth from observation of heavenly bodies, sun or stars. Clock time is available to them by virtue of their circadian rhythms, their biological clocks. A ship's navigator uses precisely these two pieces of information, time and altitude of the heavenly body, in order to fix his position on a chart; the angle of the sun or moon gives him latitude and, with a precise time, he can add his longitude. Experimentally, pigeons have been shown to make a 90° error in heading when they have had their natural day rhythm upset by six hours but they are actually able to home in overcast conditions (possibly by interpreting polarized light in ultra-violet wavelengths) and even when they have been fitted with opaque spectacles which make them effectively blind. It has been suggested that they are able to sense the Earth's magnetic field and they have been shown to do so experimentally. Even more astonishingly, they may be able to detect variations in the Earth's gravitational field, which, in relating to the passage of the lunar month, could provide them with compass clues. Pigeons have been shown to detect changes in barometric pressure, which opens up the possibility that birds may be able to forecast weather changes, including changes of wind. This also means that effectively they have an altimeter while they are flying, capable of recording changes in height of less than ten metres, a useful facility on a poor weather passage.

Another astonishing possibility is that birds are sensitive enough to low-frequency sounds to be

Above: A ringed chaffinch. In Britain, the ringing programme is organized by the British Trust of Ornithology. Over a period of years systematic research has revealed a great deal of information both about wild bird movements and life-spans. If it's lucky, a chaffinch might survive ten years. Only a small proportion of ringed birds are recovered, so every recovery is of great value.

Right: Ringing a swift. Notice the way the bird's head is firmly but gently held between the first and second fingers while the leg is held between thumb and forefinger. The special pliers form rings from strips of metal. Each ring carries a number and an address. Ringers are rigorously trained and operate under a strict permit system.

able to hear certain natural sound signals from distances of thousands of miles, using the 'sound signature' of winds on distant mountains or waves breaking on distant shores as a homing beacon or as a fixed point from which to take bearings. This presupposes that they are able to resolve Doppler shifts in apparent frequency while in flight.

What seems most likely is that birds have access to a whole range of navigational aids and that they make use of them according to the weather conditions and problems they face at any particular time. The only certain thing is that the systems work, except on the occasions when foul weather deprives them of access to information.

While swallows, untypically, migrate at almost ground level, most passerines fly at a fair height. Radar watching has shown they can achieve 14,000 feet (4,300 m) and even on occasion as much as 20,000 feet (6,100 m), a height they must reach to cross the Himalayas. I have shivered thousands of feet up in the Swiss Alps at the Col de Bretolet, watching blue tits pounding their way up the valley zigzagging from side to side, unable to fly at an angle which would take them straight up and over the pass. I suppose it was imagination but

Brent geese breed in the high arctic but visit British estuaries in winter to feed on the eel-grass of sand and mud-flats. They may also visit coastal fields to graze.

I could almost hear their sighs of relief as they reached the top and began to coast downhill to the welcoming bosom of Italy.

Swans have been recorded at heights in excess of 27,000 feet (8,200 m). They were first 'seen' by an Air Traffic Control radar unit in Northern Ireland, and then confirmed visually by the pilot of an aircraft bound for Prestwick. He reported a flock of 'about thirty swans' and the radar unit calculated that they were flying south at about seventy-five knots, though there is no record of the wind speed and direction. This represents probably the greatest height achieved by British birds.

It is typical of very large birds like swans and geese that, in any serious long-distance flying, they adopt a V-formation. There has been much controversy about what kind of benefit this brings the birds, whether there is any aerodynamic gain or whether they are simply flying in close formation so that they all stay together and do not get lost. Further controversy arises over whether

Geese in V-formation, a practice typical also of gulls. There is much controversy about the reasons for this behaviour. These are snow geese, very rare visitors to Britain.

there is one particular bird which leads or whether birds take the lead in turns. One theoretical study has shown that each bird receives a small amount of lift from the air-wave set up by the wing beat of the bird in front of it but in order for this to be effective in real-life conditions the birds would have to keep accurate station on each other in terms of both angle, distance and wing-phasing. Analysis of movie-film has shown that these requirements are simply not met and that the birds do not maintain accurate stations in flight. But since the birds do fly in formation there must be some advantage in such behaviour. It may simply be that wildfowl families need to keep together in order to pass on information about routes and stopping-off places but it is still tempting to feel that there must be some aerodynamic benefit. A small increase in efficiency would be proportionately more important to large birds, which are only able to put on a relatively small amount of extra fat before setting off on migration.

By any standards, migration journeys provide a harsh test for a bird and many never arrive at their destination. Some, of course, arrive at a place to which they never meant to go. Many American birds find themselves deposited on our shores with the unsolicited help of strong westerly winds. A few may even have had an assisted passage by courtesy of a steamship company. To the best of my knowledge, there is no truth in the mediaeval story that swallows carried a small stick when crossing the sea, so that they could use it as a temporary raft if they felt like a short rest on the way.

Year after year in real life, northward-moving warm air masses give the swallows a helpful push on their return journey in the spring. A warm March will see the arrival on our shores of the first serious numbers of summer visitors. Cock wheat-ears flash their white rumps and chiffchaffs and willow warblers bring their welcome song. Towards the end of April, the coast and the inland copses and spinneys are echoing with the songs of arriving migrants. Cuckoos and swallows, swifts and white-throats all take up positions and prepare for another session of family life.

7
The Changing Fortunes of Birds

Collared doves have successfully invaded
the British Isles.

For a small island, Britain supports a phenomenal number of birds, somewhere in the region of 120 million. Of the 430 or so species which regularly visit and could be called 'British', sixteen of them represent populations of more than a million. It is probable that the wren is the commonest breeding bird we have, found anywhere that offers a scrap of cover. The estimate is that there could be 3,000 pairs in every six mile square, resulting in a total population of ten million pairs. That figure would be seriously reduced after an icy winter but represents an average in a run of reasonable years. Blackbirds and chaffinches are nearly as numerous, with some seven million breeding pairs. Robins, blue tits and house sparrows have populations of some five million pairs apiece. There may be more than a million and a half waders on our estuaries just after Christmas, a quarter of this number in the Morecambe Bay area alone. There must be well over 150,000 pairs of gannets nesting round the British Isles, a number which is increasing all the time and which has benefited from the changes in public attitudes over the last 100 years; instead of being over-exploited for food and 'sport', the species is now held in high regard and carefully protected.

Counting birds is something of a sport in itself, much indulged in by the majority of birdwatchers, yet it is much more than a sport; it is a useful exercise that reveals a great deal of information about the general health of an environment. It was the catastrophic breeding failure of our birds of prey in the late 1950s that highlighted the dangers of toxic agricultural pesticides and led to their control.

Over the years, various techniques for estimating populations have been devised and these are the subject of continuing study, mainly by the British Trust for Ornithology. The longest-running species census involves the grey heron, whose easily-mapped and conspicuous breeding places were first counted in 1928 and are still carefully monitored every year. The observers are careful not to risk any disturbance of the colony till well into the breeding season. It is relatively easy to get a fairly accurate idea of the number of nests and young in a heronry but counting serried ranks of guillemots or kittiwakes on cliff ledges from a wildly moving boat is a different kettle of fish. Trying to count the seemingly endless crowd at a gannetry is not easy either. The most effective way seems to be to take a photograph from the air, more-or-less directly above the colony, and then laboriously to prick the white spots (each one a bird) on an enlargement, counting as you go. This method serves very well with a colony such as the one at Grassholm, in Dyfed, where the birds nest on a comparatively level island top but on the much steeper faces of, for instance, the Bass Rock, it is less easy to count the gannets.

From the counts on photographs taken at Grassholm, it has been shown that the colony has increased its numbers greatly since the birds first came to the island more than 100 years ago. In 1913, there were about 275 pairs occupying nests. By 1939, this had risen to nearly 6,000 pairs. Ten years later, the number was nearly 10,000. Another ten years saw another five thousand pairs on the island. During the great seabird census of 1969/70, Operation Seafarer, the figure was estimated at 16,128. By 1978, the figure was more than 20,000. The story is one of continual and dramatic increase, a consequence of reduced exploitation and an abundance of pelagic fish in the Celtic Sea. It will be interesting to see what will happen if the current over-fishing of mackerel continues. There is also the as yet uncalculated effect on breeding success of the recent explosion in the use of synthetic ropes, which often end up in gaily-coloured pieces in gannet's nests, there to ensnare both adults and young.

Great crested grebes and rooks have also been the subject of large-scale census work. In the case of the rook, the study was grant-aided by the Government, which wanted to know the economic significance of rooks on farmland. Wintering wildfowl populations have been studied since 1947, co-ordinated by the Wildfowl Trust and with the long-term object of conserving the stocks of this valuable resource. The other important continuing census is the BTO's Common Birds Census, started in 1962 and providing an annual account of status and distribution which is invaluable to conservationists and all who are concerned with the maintenance of a healthy and diverse wildlife population.

Food is the factor which has over-riding control in regulating the number of birds and the places where they live. A diverse food supply makes for a diversity of species. In the tropics, where there is a cornucopia of food, there exists the greatest variety of birds, whereas the harsh conditions of

Right: Wren at the nest, hungry chicks demanding attention. Probably our commonest species, with a total population of ten million pairs according to the British Trust for Ornithology.

Snowy owls find their way south to Shetland every few years when the lemming supply has failed in their sub-arctic home. They sometimes breed, but it seems there is not enough suitable food to sustain their invasion.

Waxwings explore eastern Britain in late autumn when the rowanberry crop fails them at home in Scandinavia. Some have stayed through till summer but none have yet bred, so far as we know.

the polar regions support relatively few species. On the other hand, the fishing is good in the north, so astronomical numbers of those few species make a good living. In the temperate latitudes, we inhabit a happy medium and find ourselves blessed with a fair variety of species.

The actual distribution of birds is determined by the climate, the kind of country they prefer and the extent of the competition. Unless you live in the favoured south and east, for instance, you will be lucky to hear a nightingale, yet in their own kind of country, in commons and woodland edge, in dense scrub and overgrown hedgerows, they were remarkably stable in population terms for a great many years, till the present trend towards over-tidy hedges, draining and scrub clearance began to reduce them in the 1950s. Britain is at the edge of their geographical range. They migrate from their African wintering quarters to breed in continental Europe and Asia Minor in their chosen valleys and wooded scrubby plains. They are not birds of the hills and this explains why in Britain they penetrate no further than the south-east, reaching only as far as Exeter and not into the extreme west-country or into Wales or the north of England, let alone Scotland and Ireland.

Some birds find themselves in Britain either because their food supply has failed elsewhere or because they are becoming so successful that they must spread out and colonize new countries. The famous snowy owls, which sometimes penetrate south from their sub-Arctic haunts to excite the human visitors to Shetland, arrive because their lemming supply has failed, as it does every few years. They come to sample the voles of the northernmost tip of Britain but, presumably, find that our table is not quite abundant enough to support them, so that after a few isolated breeding attempts they withdraw back to lemming country.

If the rowan berry crop fails or runs short in Scandinavia, hordes of ravenous waxwings may visit us in autumn and winter, to the delight of birdwatchers in eastern Britain. They breed from arctic Norway to Siberia but, occasionally,

Bearded tits have their British base in the reed beds of East Anglia, but increased breeding success has encouraged them to explore possibilities further south and west. Mild winters might allow an explosion in their numbers.

individuals have stayed, behind in Britain to display and sing in the spring. Perhaps one day they will breed. Bearded tits, which nest in reed-beds of the Norfolk Broads and Suffolk have been thought of as rather sedentary birds yet a series of mild winters and successful breeding seasons increased their population to a level at which even they were forced to explore further afield. Now they have established bridgeheads in small numbers at suitably reedy places along the south and east coasts. Severe winters hold them back; mild winters see them investigating reed-beds even as far west as South Devon but they withdraw east for the breeding season. Nevertheless, this is the typical pattern for an exploding species and it is the sort of behaviour that makes for fascinating birdwatching.

The mild winters and increasing warmth in the northern hemisphere which was typical of the first half of the twentieth century has favoured the prospects of spread for quite a lot of birds. Continental species have invaded not only the British Isles but have penetrated as far as Iceland in some cases. While the converse is true, with birds like snow bunting and ptarmigan retreating north, away from us, our gains have more than outweighed the losses.

Perhaps our most spectacular and unexpected immigrant was the collared dove. No common or garden birdwatcher had even heard the name of the bird when it first bred in Britain in 1955 yet in twenty-five years or so collared doves have spread to every corner of the country and consolidated their position as common residents. Their spread from India across central Europe during the 1930s and then through Germany, France and the Low Countries in the 1940s brought them to the barrier of the English Channel in the early 1950s, having steadily covered 1,000 miles in less than twenty years. The Channel proved no real obstacle and on the British side they found a countryside much to their liking, allied to a tolerant human population which welcomed them and only slowly realized that they might have thrown open their country to a pest.

Collared doves choose to establish themselves close to human habitations, especially where there is a supply of grain. Chicken runs, docksides,

137

How many gannet pairs breed on
Grassholm Island, Dyfed?
Superimposing a grid on a much
enlarged version of this aerial
photograph, several workers
laboriously counted each
individual bird sitting on a nest.
The results varied from 19,274 to
21,691, and the generally
accepted average gave a 1978
population of 20,200. Ten years
earlier there had been 16,128. The
gannetry was first occupied
somewhere around a hundred
years earlier.

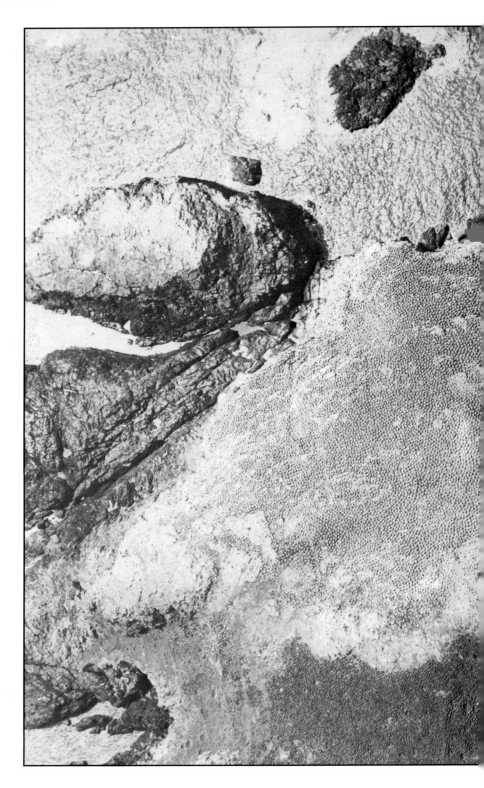

Mediterranean birds possibly invading Britain

Golden oriole

European roller

Hoopoe

Cetti's warbler

Fan-tailed warbler

Cetti's warbler is now moderately well established as a breeding bird in Britain. Will the others follow suit?

pheasant-rearing pens, parks and big gardens in suburban or village settings all suit them very well. Provided there are some evergreen trees, where they may nest and roost, they settle in happily and make themselves at home, rearing young to colonize farther afield but sitting tight themselves. With their dusty-brown bodies and half-collars of black, they are now a familiar sight and the nasal churring noise they make in flight is an equally familiar sound, to say nothing of their coo-*coo*-coo song, which sometimes leads people up the garden path, thinking they have heard a winter cuckoo.

Apart from the dramatic arrival and consolidation of the now-resident collared dove, there have been quite a number of other gains to the British list emanating from the south. Unlike the dove, the serin was confidently expected but it was a very long time finding its way from the Mediterranean fringe, where it was at home at the beginning of the nineteenth century, to Britain, where it first bred as a summer visitor in the 1970s. As a weed-seed fancier, you may find it on dockside waste ground or in the right sort of large garden in rural surroundings. Firecrests have also found their way to the south coast in ever-increasing numbers. As spruce seed specialists, they may be expected to take advantage of increased Forestry Commission activities.

Cetti's warbler is another of these recent arrivals, coming, like the serin, from the Mediterranean and taking advantage of the general amelioration of the British climate. First breeding in the early 1970s, it is now moderately well established in Kent, with outposts from south Devon to Norfolk. Like the collared dove, it is a resident, a somewhat sedentary species. At first it was thought that it would be unable to survive really severe weather, as its steady northward advance had only been delayed in response to hard winters, but the fierce cold of the winter of 1978–9 only served as a slight check to its spread.

A similarly sedentary bird and possibly the next acquisition to our list is the fan-tailed warbler. Again, a series of mild winters have encouraged it to spread north right across France to nest on the other side of the Channel from us. Single scouting birds have been seen in Norfolk and it seems highly likely that it is about to join Cetti's warbler and the others on the British breeding list. Bonelli's warbler is another name to look out for.

Other birds which have bred sporadically in southern England through the years seem to need a change of climate before they will seriously take the plunge. Exotic species like hoopoes, rollers and golden orioles need warm, dry summers to provide the abundance of grasshoppers and such-like fat insects to support them. A fine spring brings a hopeful flush of these welcome beauties overshooting the Channel to our shores but, unfortunately, the trend seems to be towards cooler springs and wetter summers, which will inevitably be a setback for them. The only bright side of this recent trend may be that our recent arctic spells have seen an improvement in the prospects for the snow buntings which so recently deserted us.

The spread of birds and, for that matter, the loss of birds is not only assisted by changes in climate. One of the major influences on their status is that of Man the tool user and his works. Although, in evolutionary terms, that influence is of recent origin, the effects have been marked, especially in a country as small as ours. When Neolithic man got the feel of an axe in his hand, the face of Britain received a rude shock. Until he acquired tools, man had been a hunter and a gatherer of fruits, nuts and vegetation but the axe gave him the power to cut down broad-leafed woodland which had flourished since the Ice Age. Slashing and burning, he cleared land to grow cereals and grass, to bake bread and nourish domesticated cattle and sheep. Man the hunter became man the farmer and gardener, dominating a landscape largely of his own creation. Britain, which was once an enormous forest, is now a cultivated land of grass and arable farms, cities and industry. A modest ten per cent of the woodland remains, giving much pleasure and interest, to say nothing of its practical contribution to a healthy ecosystem.

Many of the forest birds have found a sympathetic home alongside us in our gardens, which, at their best, represent a slice of woodland edge in ecological terms. Others have learnt to adapt to the opportunities provided by industrial works, docksides and all manner of business premises and unlikely habitats.

The loss of the forests provided benefits for many. Lapwings flourished on the new grazing. Rooks enjoyed new foraging country. Since earthworms are their principal food, along with leatherjackets, other insects and newly sown grain, they happily associated themselves with farming and followed the plough, so long as there was a clump of trees or a small wood to provide shelter for the communal rookery. Finding food in association with our works, they happily moved to

141

live alongside us, building their dwellings in close proximity to our own. Rookeries tend to be in the midst of human habitations, villages or rural townships, never far from the open country in which they forage.

Unfortunately, rooks are in decline. A survey in 1975 showed that in the British Isles their numbers had been reduced by nearly 45 per cent over the previous thirty years. The reasons are not entirely clear. Increasing urbanization is one of the factors (in the London area alone, the reduction is of some 60 per cent) but changes in agricultural practice also contribute to their decline, for there is less grassland than in the past. Possibly, climatic changes have affected them and, certainly, the loss of nest sites has disadvantaged them. The catastrophic effect of Dutch elm disease has seen the loss of many more than half of our elm trees, south of a line from the Mersey to the Wash.

Elms provided ideal nest sites for rooks. They are typical hedgerow trees, often in small spinneys and invariably associated with farming. An elm spinney alongside grassland suited the rooks perfectly, providing a place to nest and plenty of earthworms to eat. The loss of elms is bound to affect the numbers and distribution of rooks. In west Gloucestershire alone, between 1972 and 1975, the proportion of rooks' nests in elms fell from 86 to 56 per cent, while that in ash rose from 7 per cent to 26 per cent. In fact, Scots pine is their preferred nest tree when they have the option; not surprisingly, more than half the Scottish rooks nest in Scots pine and, in the most windswept parts of England, like Devon and Cornwall, these trees form important rookery sites. However, in England generally, elm is the practical alternative, with beech coming second. Rooks will, in fact, nest in sycamore, ash or oak if they must, having persevered in the dead elms for a while. They have been known to nest in giant electricity pylons and on the rungs of cooling-tower ladders but these, after all, are only tree-substitutes to the eye of a rook, somewhat analogous to the use of artificial nest boxes by tits, which simply see the boxes as convenient holes in 'trees'.

The disease which has stricken our elms may have been bad news for rooks but it has served woodpeckers well. Great spotted woodpeckers have found the infected trees a welcome source of extra food and flourished accordingly. It is certainly a mistake to cut all the elms down and tidy them up too smartly. The problem is a temporary one in any case. Unless the whole of the

root system is killed, it will throw up suckers and reproduce vegetatively, so that the hedgerows will blossom with a disease resistant strain of the tall elm yet again. That presupposes that the hedgerows themselves will not be bulldozed and destroyed in the name of agricultural progress.

Hedgerow removal obviously alters the character of a farm's bird community, though a BTO study showed that it did not seriously impoverish bird life. A Norfolk farm improved its operating success by removing a third of the hedgerow system, to enlarge the fields, and filled in ponds and felled a lot of trees at the same time. Two four-year surveys 'before and after' showed that seed-

Above: Removal of hedgerows alters the character of a farm's bird community, but does not necessarily impoverish it. Hedgerow birds will suffer; ducks, gamebirds, plovers and crows may benefit, provided there is suitable cover for them not far away.

Left: In early spring rooks repair their nests in a beech wood. Rook populations are in decline, partly because of increasing urbanization and changes in agricultural practices.

eating birds were little affected, that 'field' species like mallards, partridges, plovers and larks fared better and that only the 'hedgerow' species declined. Wrens, blackbirds, song thrushes and dunnocks lost about a quarter of their numbers but, at least, these all represent very common species. Perhaps the survey shows yet again that birds, like other animals, are more resilient than we allow. Even the stone curlew, which suffered so badly from heathland reclamation, which deprived it of its natural home in dry, open ground, has shown signs of fighting back from its sad decline. As a summer visitor at the very north-western edge of its natural range, it might have

been expected to withdraw in the face of adverse conditions. Increasing cultivation and afforestation are anathema to it, yet it has successfully colonized arable fields and found a home of sorts on those wide open firebreak strips between the orderly blocks of conifers planted by the Forestry Commission.

Corncrakes suffered from the increasing mechanization of farm work. Preferring to nest in open grass-fields, their nests and eggs and sometimes even they themselves (since they are so reluctant to flush) are destroyed by the unseeing blades of the hay cutter. In the old days, a man wielding a scythe was able to see them in time to spare them.

Nowadays, with the increasing tendency towards silage making, the grass fields are not only cut earlier in the year but cut more often, so that the hard-pressed corncrake is holding on only by its beak, in the extreme west and north. In 1978, a survey estimated that there were probably no more than 650 calling males in Scotland, England and Wales, most of them in the Hebrides, where they patronize marshy meadows. The only bright sign for the species is that Irish corncrakes have taken to breeding on waste ground by factories and show some interest in colonizing suburbia.

Drainage and water schemes of all sorts have had major effects on bird numbers and fortunes. Farmers and water engineers have been busily draining marshes for the last hundred years or so with increased intensity, and water birds have suffered accordingly. Marsh harriers went into a decline from which they have never recovered, although they enjoyed a temporary respite when war-time flooding gave them a foothold in the coastal marshes of Suffolk. Quite apart from the loss of feeding habitat which resulted from drainage schemes, they had been under a lot of

Above: Reversing the tide. At Minsmere the RSPB has created a highly attractive feeding and nesting area for seabirds, ducks and waders. Shallow and insect-rich lagoons are dotted with low-lying islands. Large numbers of birds feed and breed here.

Right, above: Waders congregate in large numbers. These are dunlin, with a few black-headed gulls and oystercatchers.

Right, below: Birdwatchers sometimes congregate in large numbers, too.

pressure from egg collectors. Now, with perhaps half a dozen breeding pairs in the whole of Britain, their status is highly precarious, but improving.

Fortunately for the harriers, their tiny hold is centred on the Minsmere reserve of the RSPB, where the extensive reed-beds over which they hunt are carefully maintained, but the long-term prospects for any bird are not healthy if they must rely on protection. From everyone's point of view, the best solution is to manage a landscape which not only provides food for people but which sustains a large and diverse population of birds. Having said that, there is no doubt that the reserve activities of an enlightened bird society, like the RSPB, can have significant effects on the birds of

an area. In the long run, I suspect that their educational activities will be the most significant but that is another story.

The greatest achievement of the RSPB in terms of rare-bird rehabilitation is their continuing success with the avocet, an elegant fowl which had become extinct in England in the first half of the nineteenth century as a result of coastal and marsh drainage and the exploitation of their eggs for the market. Always a favourite wader with all birdwatchers, its numbers increased mightily in the Netherlands and Denmark when breeding sites were improved and protected in the 1930s. In late summer and autumn, there are concentrations of some 25,000 avocets. Wartime flooding in East Anglia (in the interests of protection against invasion) provided the right conditions of shallow coastal lagoons for breeding, and encouraged some scouting pioneers to try nesting again in Suffolk after odd pairs had tried to recolonize Essex and possibly Norfolk.

Once the first avocets had bred successfully, a small group of birdwatching enthusiasts grew into a mighty band dedicated to encouraging the birds to consolidate their gains. As the years went by, they increased the breeding population by farming the land for avocet-production. They created a bird-rich lagoon, furnished with special low-lying 'scrape' islands, by using birdwatcher labour and bulldozers, turning their Minsmere reserve into the most dramatic summer bird spectacle in Britain. Since those early post-war years, when every egg hatched was hot news, the population has risen steadily, so that now 150 pairs of avocets, spread over three sites, annually rear some 100 chicks. Parallel with that success, the avocets have chosen to winter in increasing numbers on the Tamar and Exe estuaries in Devon, where they brighten the west-country winter. One of the pleasures of December is the yearly cruise in a pleasure boat, when members of the RSPB and other keen birdwatchers join me in hopes of a good view of these beautiful long-legged birds, the cream of birdwatching.

Above: Ruddy ducks in courtship display. These stiff-tails come from North America, escaped birds have bred successfully in the wild and are now an established part of the British bird scene. In autumn they flock to reservoirs in the Midlands.

Left: Flooded gravel pits offer a welcome new habitat for water birds such as grebes, moorhens and many others.

It has to be recognized that the act of bird-watching can on occasion be to the disadvantage of birds, by disturbing them at breeding and feeding grounds. The sight of a party of rarity hunters, anxious to tick off a new bird on their 'life-list' may not be a pretty one when a farmer sees his hedges torn down and his growing crops trampled. The much beleaguered Dartford warbler, hanging on precariously in the gorsy heathland of the central south coast, can do without the coach-loads of gawping bird tourists who come to chivvy it from bush to bush to get a good look at the bird, thus depriving it of feeding time. Photographers, too, bear a heavy responsibility when they set up hides at nests or sit tight in the middle of a bird's feeding territory. Our first duty must be to consider the welfare of the bird, before our pleasure or even our livelihood.

Holiday makers, ignorant or indifferent to the needs of birds, often cause problems. Both ringed plovers and oystercatchers increasingly find their nesting places invaded by people wishing to enjoy remote seashores. For many years, the more sociable terns suffered because of disturbance, so that nowadays they have retreated to breed on reserves or very remote islands. Oystercatchers have even begun to nest on saltmarshes but one wonders how long it will be before estuary mud and saltmarsh, among the last truly wild remnants of ancient Britain, succumb to the pressures of increasing leisure activity.

Ringed plovers, too, suffer from their breeding season coinciding with the holiday season. With the best will in the world, the trampling beach-comber does not see the saucer nest, even after he has crushed the well-camouflaged eggs. Many a time, I have seen picnic parties settle down for the afternoon near enough to eggs to force the incubating bird to leave them, or near enough to drive a parent frantic with 'injury' feigning which totally fails to lure the intruders away from young chicks just out of the nest. In response to such pressure, ringed plovers, too, are changing their habits, nesting on farmland the other side of the seawall or in the well-guarded precincts of power stations and oil refineries. Ringed plovers are not yet rare but their cousin, the Kentish plover, is decidedly so. Having become completely extinct in mainland Britain a couple of decades ago, it is making a very tentative come-back on the east-coast, away from the disturbance by Kentish holiday-makers which may have been one of the factors which caused it to desert us.

It is very easy to list the detrimental side of man's activities and the ways in which he works against the general well-being of birds. Urbanization and industrial 'improvement' reduce the supply of wild habitats. Disturbance reduces breeding success and pollution kills. Drainage of marshes and water meadows, the in-filling of bogs and ponds, all adversely affect the existence of water birds, for wetlands are particularly vulnerable to violent change. Yet there is another side to the coin. Man's activities are often favourable to bird life, even though they may not be consciously motivated in that direction.

Man-made wetlands, such as gravel and clay pits, provide excellent feeding and breeding places for a host of water and water-related birds and the ornamental ponds and lakes of our parks and gardens serve an additional purpose. Even the deep and comparatively sterile waters of reservoirs serve a useful function as a safe resting place for large numbers of waterfowl and gulls, though public health officials may not be so keen on the associated risk of bird-borne infection. The string of reservoirs ringing London has always provided rarity hunters with good birding. Indeed, there is a greater variety of waterfowl about on our waters than there was in Victorian times.

The climate, in the sense both of weather and of public opinion, has helped. People are more favourably disposed towards birds than they have been for many years. We may enjoy not only grebes, everyday ducks and gulls of the man-made lakes and reservoirs but also a number of exotic imports. The robustly named ruddy duck is a North American bird but, having escaped from captivity in the Wildfowl Trust's collection in the late 1950s, a number of pairs have bred successfully on the quiet freshwater lakes and pools and seem set fair to become an established part of our bird fauna. In the autumn they tend to concentrate as flocks of 200 or 300 on reservoirs through the Midlands from Avon to Cheshire.

Ruddy ducks became acclimatized after escaping by mistake but other wildfowl have been deliberately introduced with the misguided intention of improving our bird scene. The process began in the eighteenth century when the landed gentry took to landscaping parks and gardens. A lake or pond was an important part of the creative process and no lake was complete without a pair of noble swans and some colourful waterfowl. Inevitably, the gentlemen strove to out-Jones each other and someone brought home a breeding pair of Egyptian geese to decorate the water in much the same way as fallow deer were imported to grace the grassy vistas of the park. Egyptian geese have established feral breeding stocks only in a few locations, notably in Norfolk, but the Canada goose, introduced at much the same time and for the same reason, is known to all as a common feral goose which has been breeding wild all over England, a fair part of Wales and with outposts in Scotland for some decades. It enjoys popular protection in city parks and places like gravel pits and semi-natural reservoirs.

Pied wagtails enjoy the peace and quiet of a sewage farm. Here they are roosting on the arms which revolve over the filter beds.

Sewage farms may not sound the perfect places to spend a happy day but they are very rewarding in bird terms. Pied wagtails and starlings flock to them in large numbers to roost and to enjoy the slight warmth generated by the bacterial action at the filter beds. By day, they are joined by yellow wagtails, reed buntings and chaffinches in search of flies and worms which also enjoy the amenities. One of the more bizarre sights at the sewage works is to watch starlings jump gracefully over the revolving arms, which spray liquid from the sediment tanks onto the granite chippings of the filter beds, each time an arm threatens to spray the bird and knock it on the head at the same time. After passing through the filter beds, the cleansed liquid finds its way onto broad irrigation meadows at many sewage works; these marshy places support large numbers of birds. Reed buntings nest enthusiastically in the reedy margins; sedge and reed warblers also take advantage of the *Phragmites* beds; mallards and moorhens may find a home here as well. Thirty-one species have been known to breed at sewage farms; a further seventy-four visit them for food or peace and quiet at various times, generously tolerated by the works officials and appreciated by the bird-watchers.

Birds have been exploited vigorously by man ever since he realized that they and their eggs were good to eat but the widespread availability of the shotgun in the nineteenth century introduced a sporting era which, over the years, has had a devastating effect on one particular group, the birds of prey. Landlords began to manage their estates with the object of producing large numbers of pheasants and grouse. Gamekeepers, charged with the job of rearing the maximum number of

birds (and their competence being judged by the size of the annual 'bag') took an almost paranoiac attitude to any species which they believed, rightly or wrongly, to be detrimental to their birds. The shotgun, with its cheap supply of cartridges, gave them the power to kill 'vermin' in uncountable numbers. Foxes, stoats, weasels, eagles, buzzards, harriers, owls and crows all fell to the keeper and often enough were displayed on his 'gibbet' for all to see as proof of his diligence.

Writing in the 1850s, the Reverend F. O. Morris, a great bird popularizer and scourge of the gamekeeper, raised no objection in principle to game preserves and shooting (he well understood the concept of conservation) but did not think that gamekeepers were the best judges as to which animals did harm and which did not. He railed against 'rows of defunct hawks' on gibbets, despite the prevailing wisdom that if birds were not firmly held in check by fair means or foul they would multiply to take over the world. Morris had a long and hard struggle in rousing public feeling and

An old-style gamekeeper with the fruit of his labour—the gibbet.

Above: Peregrines have suffered greatly from human persecution. Illegally taken by would-be falconers, this bird will, with luck, be successfully returned to the wild by the RSPB.

Left: Petworth House, Sussex. No grand eighteenth-century estate was complete without a lake and introduced Canada geese.

influencing opinion in favour of protective legislation.

Apart from the shotgun, the most iniquitous device for controlling 'bird vermin' was the pole trap, in which a rabbit gin was set on top of a suitably placed pole where sparrowhawks, kestrels, owls and crows might be expected to perch. Gamekeepers used the pole trap (and, regrettably, on occasion, still do) in the mistaken belief that they were thus protecting their pheasant chicks. In fact, on a well-managed estate, only a very small percentage of the chicks will be taken by raptors and those mainly by young birds learning their trade. Inevitably, pheasant rearing encouraged a biased view of any potential threat, especially as it represents an extravagantly expensive way of rearing game birds for sport. On the credit side, the outdated kind of keeper who shot any predator, believing this to be in the best interests of his charges, is himself dying out, to be succeeded by generations of keepers with a greater understanding of the principles of game management and the more positive and productive concept of

Remains of a blackbird in the obnoxious and illegal pole trap.

It is not easy for laymen to distinguish between shag and cormorant beaks. The shag is on the left, the cormorant, with its white throat patch, on the right.

conservation, which operates to the advantage of sportsman, birdwatcher and birds alike.

Nevertheless, there is no room for complacency. In spite of fairly comprehensive legal protection, birds of prey still get shot, trapped and poisoned in unacceptable numbers. In 1980, more than ninety cases of poisoning were reported to the RSPB in the six months of summer. These cases involved golden eagles, kites and hen harriers amongst other birds. On fishing beats, some keepers still hold to the Victorian idea that 'if it eats fish, it must be bad'. Birds like cormorants are still persecuted, in spite of the well-proven fact that as predators they actually have a *beneficial* effect on prey species by reinforcing natural selection and extracting slow, sick or injured individuals from a population.

Not many years ago, in my own experience, the then Devon River Board paid a bounty on cormorant beaks delivered to its offices in Exeter. This ignorant procedure was brought to an end in the late 1950s, not by a realization that the bounty served no useful purpose in the matter of improving fishermen's catches but because we of the Devon Bird Society pointed out that they were unknowingly paying bounties on the beaks of shags. Although the shags were entirely blameless (in that they never set foot in the river water, as opposed to the salt estuary water), they nevertheless have the misfortune to carry beaks which are more-or-less indistinguishable from those of the cormorant; moreover they were a great deal easier for bounty hunters to shoot in bulk. On closer investigation, it did indeed turn out that the authorities were spending our money on shag beaks.

Peregrine falcons have suffered greatly from human persecution over the years. In Victorian times, the peregrine, much prized by falconers, fetched £1,000, a very considerable sum at that time. Curiously, peregrine's eggs today are said to be worth £1,000 in the illegal market, while the bird itself is said to fetch £1,500; this must be one of the few instances of successful resistance to inflation. Having gone into serious decline, this magnificent raptor, the fastest British falcon, picked up and began to do well in the healthier public climate of the twentieth century. There seemed hope that this species, which can date regular occupancy of its traditional cliff eyries back to mediaeval times, would have an assured future but, in war-time Britain, the peregrines were systematically shot, on official orders, because of

Motor vehicles and railway trains have taken a huge toll of barn owls' lives. Loss of habitat and a reduction in suitable nest-places has helped accelerate their decline.

The dead rabbit was baited with poison, probably meant for foxes, but the victim was a marsh harrier, an exceedingly rare bird.

the danger that they would kill message-carrying pigeons on their way back across the sea to their lofts.

By the end of the war, the peregrine population was much reduced but, when persecution was halted, the number of birds began to recover, only to be hit hard by the toxic chemicals introduced for the benefit of farmers in the late 1950s. Accumulating these poisons after feeding on sick prey, they concentrated them in their own eggs, which either proved infertile or cracked as a consequence of abnormally thin shells. Many peregrines and other birds died in pitiful circumstances but their deaths served to reveal the dangers of organo-chlorine pesticides, which were eventually subjected to a partial ban. As a result, peregrines are currently recovering in numbers, although the situation is far from satisfactory.

Owls, preying on a diet which in fact consists mainly of voles, shrews and mice, have also suffered greatly at the hands of man, partly because, like all birds of prey, they were thought to reduce game-bird populations but also because, more darkly, they have always been regarded with great suspicion as birds of evil omen. In particular, the barn owl, shrieking its way through the dusk

and with a logical predilection for vole-rich graveyards, has been killed on sight by the ignorant. Roads and railways have also taken a huge toll. In fact, barn owls are part of an almost entirely useful family from the point of view of man; at least farmers have appreciated their value in the past, including custom-built barn owl holes in their barns to encourage these rodent eaters. Loss of habitat, in the form of the rough 'waste' ground which is now cultivable by modern techniques, has hit them badly, along with a run of severe winters which reduced their prey species. Like the peregrines and other birds of prey, they, too, were badly knocked by the toxic chemicals. Barn owls have been steadily declining for the last century and the story is not much brighter for the tawny owl of park and woodland.

The extensive loss of nest-sites has also been a factor in the decline of owls. Hedgerow elms, in particular, provided exactly the sort of nest-hole which both tawny and barn owls find attractive. When branches fall from mature elms, the remnant stub-end rots out in the weather to form deep and well-drained holes. Other trees do not rot in such a helpful manner. Since farmers, nowadays are less attuned to the need for providing owl nest-boxes, this is one way in which bird enthusiasts can provide something of practical value to some of our more life-enhancing species.

Above: Rose-ringed parakeets escaped from, or were released by, cage-bird fanciers. Now they have established themselves as a feral breeding population in the south east.

Below: Huge numbers of guillemots have suffered from oil pollution, and only a small proportion are successfully rehabilitated with the help of the RSPCA.

The little owl, like its nocturnal relations, is noticeably scarcer nowadays; this also is a consequence of cold winters and farm chemicals. Unlike the other owls mentioned, it was not originally a British bird. It was first introduced from its natural habitat in Continental Europe by the eccentric naturalist Charles Waterton, in 1842. This attempt to 'improve' the British 'list' failed but subsequent re-introductions by Lord Lilford into the open farmland of Northamptonshire in the last decade of the nineteenth century slowly took a hold. Encouraged by yet more stock imported from Holland, the birds spread to almost the whole of England before their recent decline.

Other introductions, apart from the many species of wildfowl, have also enjoyed some success. Aviculturalists were responsible for the introduction of the rose-ringed parakeet, a bird whose natural home is from North Africa east through India to Burma, but these people then became less than enchanted with the species and tended to leave the window as well as the cage door open. Though they are cheap and very colourful parrots, with crimson bills, yellow-green plumage and long tails, they are somewhat unresponsive as pets, so their owners tend to lose interest when they find it difficult to make friends with them. Through the years, the rose-ringed parakeets have managed to establish some wild footholds in wooded parks in the Thames Valley and Kent area. Although it was assumed that hard winters would reduce their numbers, they seem to be more than holding their own, helped greatly by bird table provisions such as peanuts, fruit and seeds in their suburban habitats. Happily taking over woodpeckers nest holes, they seem to be in the lucky position of suffering from no obvious predator. If they do succeed and enlarge their range, the danger is that they will become a pest in the Kentish fruit farms, so it is likely that some control measures may have to be introduced.

There is no doubt that the provision of food in the garden feeding-stations has a great influence on bird numbers and variety, especially in the vast suburban sprawls around towns and big cities. Mainly, the species involved are those which had their natural home in the much-depleted woodlands of ancient Britain. They were birds of the woodland edge, feeding and nesting in the trees, foraging over the scrub and open patches for seeds and insects. Now, they take happily to the bird tables and nut baskets of well-disposed householders and breed either in creeper-clad walls or the dense hedges which divide one man's 'estate' from the next. In return, they provide entertainment and a form of companionship.

As time goes by, it is reasonable to suppose that more and yet more species will recognize the opportunity and take advantage. Already it is perfectly possible to record over forty species in your own garden, especially if you live in the climatically favoured south. In recent years, great spotted woodpeckers have learnt to come to bird tables where there is suet on offer. Even reed buntings may show their faces. Over the last twenty years, siskins, small aerobatic finches, have made spectacular progress south from their traditional wintering and breeding areas in Scotland, where they found their seed food in the pine forests. Extensive conifer plantations have encouraged them to move into the south and the discovery of easy peanut-pickings in gardens allowed them to make the instant leap from being a somewhat shy and retiring creature to being one of the bird-garden crowd, fighting it out at the nut-container with the best of them.

Bird gardeners tend to approve most of the colourful and 'well-behaved' visitors and have a special affection for their resident robin and blue-tits, even though in reality the garden robin is quite likely to be a different individual every year and the garden blue tits are represented by constantly-changing small parties of birds which are passing by on their daily pilgrimage to a quite widespread

Magpies are increasingly birds of the town and suburbs. They are adept at discovering and eating the eggs from small birds' nests.

number of potential feeding spots, a kind of avian pub crawl.

On the whole, people like least the noisy and overpowering gangs of starlings and sparrows and the larger crows or gulls which 'bully' the smaller or less aggressive birds. The more that people learn of the comings and goings of garden birds, the more tolerant they become, until they can view with equanimity the perfectly proper visit of the sparrowhawk. Even then, they are less sanguine about the marauding crow. Magpies, in particular, arouse people's ire, when they see how successful they are at stealing small birds' eggs and, often enough, the small birds themselves. It is not easy to adjust to the sight of a predator acting out its proper function. Magpies were birds of open pastureland but, with an increasing acreage going under the plough and their release from the worst excesses of the gamekeeper and poisoned bait, they have taken happily to a new style of living in urban and suburban areas. Although many people feel that they should start acting the gamekeeper in their own gardens, it may be best to allow the birds themselves to resolve their disputes.

House sparrows make a good living as parasites on suburban man, having moved away from the town centres, where, in Elizabethan England, red kites were common scavengers. In those centres, we now see gulls doing the same job, in company with feral pigeons. Nesting on the window-ledges of tower blocks, kestrels find good hunting in city parks, waste-ground and rubbish tips. Birds may undergo a sea-change in towns to become almost different creatures. The woodpigeon, which is such a wary and gun-shy bird in open country, becomes an easy-going lawn and park bird. Towns would be duller places without the companionable numbers of pigeons of all kinds, from wood-pigeons through feral pigeons to the newly arrived collared dove with its persistent calling.

The feral pigeons are a mixed bunch. Many come from superb racing-pigeon stock, birds which for one reason or another have opted out of the race; others have their genetic origins further back in the mediaeval past, when they hailed from dovecotes. All of them owe their distant origins to the truly wild rock dove, a much-reduced species of the coastal cliffs. Another species which began as a bird of the sea cliffs, although it also bred on continental mountain scree and in towns, is the black redstart, a spectacular looking bird with a very dark head and back contrasted with a startling bright orange tail. It, too, has found its way to the grimiest of British city centres, though in tiny numbers. It first arrived in Sussex in 1923, as a natural consequence of range expansion, and slowly established a bridgehead in the south-east, reaching London three years later. Possibly, the city-centre warmth helped but the arrival of war and the generous supply of suitable nesting places in the shape of bomb sites gave it a real boost, so that as many as a couple of dozen were breeding happily during the blitz years. This honeymoon period did not last, fortunately for the rest of us, and, in the years since the war, the black redstart has had to cast around for alternative accommodation; it has found it, naturally enough, at sites on the sea cliffs but also at other man-made places such as power stations, so that its population currently stands at some thirty pairs. The species has an outlying presence up the east coast and into the midlands. If it can only find an acceptable urban version of stony mountain country, perhaps it may increase. In the meantime, it would be good to see it more firmly established on the coast.

Swallows and swifts are both birds which presumably originated from cliffs but have found a convenient home on and in our houses. Once you begin to see factory and high-rise buildings as man-made versions of sea-cliffs, it comes as no surprise to see wild sea-going birds like the kittiwake comfortably established in serried ranks along the waterside windows in Newcastle.

Kittiwakes do not find their food in towns but other gulls have for many years taken the opportunities provided by friendly people and by the ever-increasing tide of waste which we conveniently tip onto the ground. Reservoirs provide excellent, safe roosting places and buildings provide breeding places, so gulls are well content to increase their population at our expense. Their habit of nesting on roof tops dates back to the beginning of this century but became established in the 1920s in the south-west, spreading steadily throughout the country. Today, the habit is widespread, though in numerical terms it is insignificant by comparison with the number of gulls nesting in the more traditional manner. The roof sites suit them well, though. They like to be *by* something and build against a chimney pot or similar out-thrust. Safely out of everyone's way and relatively unbothered by the great black-backs which take their chicks, the herring gulls have a greater breeding success when they nest on roof tops, so it is a safe bet that the

Kittiwakes are sea-going gulls, but they must come ashore to breed. Their nests are plastered to the sheer cliff-face in what appears a precarious manner, but works perfectly. About half a million pairs breed in Britain and their numbers are steadily increasing.

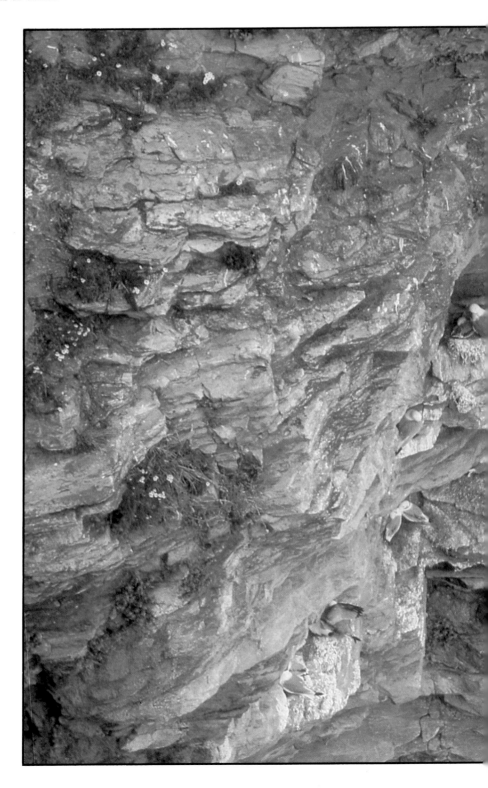

Kittiwakes are increasingly taking advantage of man-made sites such as window-ledges on waterside warehouses. These found a noble setting on a now demolished hotel in Lowestoft.

habit will continue and become even more common, to the detriment of a lot of people's peace and quiet.

Gulls are not the only birds which have taken to the roof tops. Terns have tried it, to say nothing of pigeons, oystercatchers and ospreys (in the USA). A raven even set up home on the top of Swansea Guildhall.

Fulmars have now begun to colonize buildings, which is no great surprise, since this is a bird with an explosive capacity for enlarging its sphere of influence. A hundred years ago it was confined (in its British presence) to the remote island of St Kilda. Now it has taken over the coast of Britain, nesting anywhere that offers a suitable ledge, though its hold is strongest on Atlantic-facing cliffs. On the coast of Norfolk, where the sheer cliffs lack flat places, the boys of Gresham's School put up 'nest boxes' in the form of flat wooden ledges, which were promptly colonized by the fulmars.

The spread of the fulmars was almost certainly fuelled by man's activities. Though the gradual warming of the North Atlantic over the last century may have helped, the increase in fulmars round the North Atlantic seaboard has been paralleled firstly by the increase in whaling, then by an increase in the trawling industry. Both activities provide vast quantities of the offal which fulmars enjoy, though it is probably not their favourite food.

While many species do well by taking advantage

Herring gulls are opportunist and adaptable. They have been nesting on rooftops since the 1920s, with great breeding success. Rooftops are safe places, food is rarely far away.

of our works, others suffer. Huge numbers of auks, mostly guillemots, have perished as a direct result of increasing oil tanker traffic in the world's oceans. Swimming into oil slicks, their feathers become clogged and their lungs burned. It is not at all clear, however, that oil pollution is a significant factor in the undoubted changes in auk distribution. The birds have been retreating north since the beginning of this century, possibly as a natural consequence of some change in the availability of their fish prey. The increase in number of gulls may also have had its effect, since gulls are active predators on auks and auk eggs. Perhaps, if conditions change, the puffins will return to the south coast and the Bristol Channel islands which were once their natural home.

Fluctuations in bird fortunes are clearly part of the natural scheme of things. While men may influence, sometimes greatly, the stocks and behaviour of a bird, natural phenomena can be more constructive by far, and, inevitably, on occasion, vastly more destructive. Long-term climatic changes force a species inexorably either to expand or to contract its range. Wrynecks, almost common 100 years ago, are near extinction in England. The same is true of red-backed shrikes. We must be grateful, therefore, for the return of the avocet, the black-tailed godwit and the osprey, while we reflect that extinction is the inevitable long-term prospect for every species, when it is succeeded in time by those better-fitted to fill its particular niche.

8
Exploitation of Birds

Pigeon-baskets on a transporter.

Flegg-netting in the Hebrides, a nineteenth-century print. Islanders have harvested their seabird colonies for centuries with success. Properly managed, the bird populations are unharmed.

As we have seen, man has had a profound effect on bird fortunes. Farming activities alter the balance of a landscape; towns, cities, industry and the communications network alter its physical make-up, with inevitable consequences for bird populations both in terms of species and numbers. But man's most direct influence has been in his ceaseless efforts to use birds for food.

The flesh of birds is good to eat and so are their eggs. We know that the earliest men took advantage of this food source, since their middens are well supplied with bird bones. Doubtless, they hunted birds with all the ingenuity they could muster and, as the years went by, they progressed from straightforward stone-throwing and egg-stealing to a whole battery of weapons designed to capture birds.

By the seventeenth century, Francis Willughby was able to describe in detail the various 'engines and devices' used by the ardent fowler. As well as animal aids, like hawks and dogs, he used nets, springs, snares, traps, pitfalls, guns, cross-bows, birdlime and baits. Most of these methods had been available for a long time; some date back to prehistory. All of them are now illegal except in certain clearly defined circumstances.

Small birds were much in demand for the pot until comparatively recently. Sparrows and yellowhammers were regarded as 'good eating'; starlings were 'good to eat but slightly bitter'. Thrushes of all sorts were commonly sold at markets throughout Britain. Liming was a particularly messy way of immobilizing small perching birds but it was certainly known to the Romans and was probably in use long before their time. Holly bark and twigs were boiled for some time and pounded with some corn and possibly some

Clap-netting in ancient Egypt.

The result of 'liming'. This nightingale is firmly stuck to a twig, but is still alive.

goose-grease. The sticky result of this mixture was spread along likely branches at a roosting place, with the object of catching birds at night time. A variation on this method was to attract small birds to a well-limed bush during the day by 'hiding' a decoy-owl inside it, thereby inducing them to mob it and so get their feathers smeared in the process, so that they could not fly properly.

Bat-fowling was a nocturnal pursuit but with birds, not bats, as the quarry. The fowlers were instructed to take a vessel with fire in it, accompanied by men carrying poles with bundles of dry straw or hay bound to the top. Yet more men carried poles with which to beat the roosting bushes and trees when their fellows lit their torches and attacked the birds with them. The birds were expected to rise in the pitch darkness and play about the flames 'so that they who do have the poles may at their pleasure strike them down and take them'. At the same time, a well-limed bush made of birch or willow was placed nearby, with a blazing torch to attract birds to settle on it.

Liming was a cheap and fairly effective method of capturing small birds but trapping techniques were much improved with time. Some of the more effective clap-nets and cage-traps are still in use,

notably by bird ringers at observatories. The famous Heligoland trap, which provides attractive bushes in an otherwise bare landscape in order to lure migrating birds into a cage, was first developed by continental bird-fowlers seeking thrushes and songbirds in general but it now has an honourable place in the history of migration research. It has been used to capture countless thousands of birds whose vital statistics are recorded before they are sent on their way, identified by a small metal band on their feet. A more recent variation on this method of trapping has been the development of rocket netting, where the net may be deployed anywhere from a goose ground or wader roost to a refuse dump patronized by gulls.

Geese are particularly vulnerable to capture after the breeding season, when they must endure a period of flightlessness while they moult to a new suit of feathers. At this time, it is possible to herd them into enclosures. Earlier in the season, those people fortunate enough to live near breeding geese would have had the opportunity to take

In medieval times no one knew
where barnacle geese bred.
Convenient myths allowed their
classification as fish, permitting
them to be eaten on Friday without
a guilty conscience.

eggs or young suitable for fattening. On their wintering grounds, the flocks of both swans and geese would have been harried by snaring and trapping. With the more widespread availability of the shotgun, enormous numbers were taken, until many traditional goose grounds were completely cleared; only the most remote and inaccessible survived. Legal protection arrived only just in time to bring the chance of more constructive management of the valuable resource.

Greylags have always been the species most hunted in Britain, though the other geese also found their way to the table. The barnacle goose

Above: Birth of barnacle geese. 'Certain trees bear fruit which . . . produces a worm which . . . flies like a bird.'

Right: Bird-trapping techniques as illustrated in Willughby's *Ornithology*, 1678.

has a curious claim to fame in this regard. In early times, no one knew where the birds bred; their arrival every autumn was regarded as something of a mystery, explained only by a bizarre link with a marine crustacean, the goose barnacle. The geese arrived on our shores at about the time of the September gales, the time when large-scale stranding of the barnacles occurs. Commonly thrown ashore attached to floating branches or driftwood, goose barnacles do bear a striking resemblance to the neck and beak of a bird, complete with 'feathers' in the shape of their filter mechanisms, the *cirri*.

The popular myth held that no egg or nest was involved in the development of the bird but that the infant stage of the barnacle geese was generated spontaneously and nourished by trees: 'Certain trees bear fruit which, decaying within, produces a worm which, as it subsequently develops, becomes hairy and feathered, and, provided wings, flies like a bird.' At a time when dietary laws were more closely followed by the religious, the advantage of believing in the maritime origin of the fat bird was obvious. Coming from the sea, the barnacle goose could be safely classified as a fish, suitable for the table on a Friday. The tradition flourished till the Pope forbade the practice by decree in the twelfth century but it lingered for several centuries more in the remoter parts of Ireland.

Wild ducks congregate in large numbers for migrations and at the winter feeding places and they have always been highly-prized for the table. In the days before deep freezes and intensive agriculture made us almost independent of the seasons, the arrival of airborne meat, flying in with the onset of hard weather, must have seemed a miraculous convenience but wild ducks are wary birds, not at all easy to catch. Through the years, they have successfully weathered all forms of trap, ambush, decoy, punt-gun and shotgun and still visit us in large numbers every winter. Whether the wildfowl are taken for the pot or in the name of sport, the abiding principles of harvesting must be honoured: only the excess of the crop may be taken or there is a risk of long-term damage to the population. Wildfowl represent a natural resource just as surely as do the farmer's fields of cereal or the forester's trees or the fisherman's fish.

Before the large-scale introduction of guns, the best way of catching ducks was to use traps. Of all the trapping methods, the most successful has been the pipe-decoy. Dating back to the sixteenth

A Trap Cage for Night ingales.

The Pantiere Nett.

The Sparrow Nett.

Catching birds with a Setting Dog, and Nett.

A Tunnelling Nett for Partridge.

Tunnelling for Quails.

century, at one time there were as many as two hundred in operation in Britain. Even today, several are still in use, in the service of bird ringing for scientific research. At the New Grounds, in Gloucestershire, Sir Peter Scott's Wildfowl Trust has a fine example and there is another at Abbotsbury in Dorset, operated by the swanherd, John Fair. At Orielton, in Pembrokeshire, the Field Studies Council now have the remains of a once active decoy. I have spent many happy hours patching the netting, in the hope of trapping and ringing a few wigeon or teal or mallard. In the old days, the birds were captured for the kitchen.

The decoy involved a lake or pond, sometimes man-made, surrounded by quiet, undisturbed woodland. From the open water, radiated several ditches, leading off into the vegetation. The ditches were enclosed with funnel-nets, stretched over hoops, and these 'pipes' tapered as the ditch curved to a dead end. Tame decoy ducks dabbled

Pipe decoy of a type which dates back to the sixteenth century. The wild ducks, encouraged by a 'judas', are swimming towards the dog in order to harass it. The man is concealed behind the screens while the dog shows itself in brief sorties.

inside the pipe, feeding on the corn provided, to attract the wild ducks to join them. Screens of reeds prevented the ducks from seeing the decoyman and his dog, a vital assistant. When the trained dog showed himself at the entrance to the pipe, the nearest ducks would react in a manner typical of their tribe: they would 'mob' him in much the same way that small birds will harass an owl. The dog showed himself briefly in carefully arranged gaps in the reed screen, each time leading the ducks deeper into the narrowing pipe. At the critical moment, the decoyman showed himself at the pipe entrance and the ducks flew away from him in panic, towards the dead end of the funnel, thus finding themselves trapped in the purse net. The 'Judas' ducks, meanwhile, stayed quietly in the pipe, unafraid of the man. One of the cunning advantages of the system was that the whole operation could be carried out without disturbing the main flock of ducks which remained on the open pond; the decoyman could make several catches from the same flight of duck.

In one season, 31,200 ducks, including teal and wigeon, were sent to London from the decoys in Lincolnshire. The trade was licensed by Act of

Parliament. One of the reasons for legal control was to protect birds breeding in this country. At one summer drive, timed when the young ducklings had not quite got their flight feathers, no less than 3,000 ducks are said to have been bagged. Francis Willughby tells of a drive in which 400 boats on Deeping Fen took 4,000 fat ducklings. This sort of harvesting seemed likely to harm the stock and therefore to be bad for trade, so an Act of Parliament in 1534 established a close season protecting wildfowl between 31 May and 31 August. Winter decoying was licensed from late October through to February. Wildfowling for ducks and geese, and wader hunting too, is strictly controlled to this day in all European countries and, even more strictly, in North America. Close seasons protect the breeding stock and a system of quotas or protected areas seeks to regulate the numbers taken in winter in such a way that the populations of the various species are maintained at healthy levels.

Besides ducks and geese, man has lived off other birds which not only congregate in large numbers but are relatively easy to harvest. From the plentiful supply of bones in prehistoric middens,

Above: Waterfowl congregate in large numbers in winter, a time when they were particularly welcome as a food source.

Below: 'Sledging' across wet mud in pursuit of wildfowl with a punt gun. Aquatint by Henry Alken, *c*. 1800.

we can say with certainty that early man not only ate waterfowl and gamebirds but that he sampled seabirds like auks and gannets. To this day, the annual gatherings of breeding seabirds provide remote islanders with a welcome addition to the larder but islanders have always been forced by circumstance to take greater care of their precious food resources than the profligate mainlanders, who have over-exploited wild stocks all over the world.

The islanders of Iceland, the Faeroes and the remoter Hebrides harvested their seabird visitors over thousands of years in ways which ensured long-term enjoyment of the food they represented. They learnt, the hard way, that it was safe to take more than half of the eggs laid by the guillemots at first laying, because, provided the season was young enough, the females would lay again to replace their single egg. The auks were then left undisturbed. The islanders took their tithe of fat young fulmars and gannets just before they flew the nest, much later in the summer. Acting as natural predators, they left the breeding hordes no worse off than when they came.

Fulmars have been taken in enormous numbers from the seabird cliffs to the north of Britain but, until the late nineteenth century, the remote island community of St Kilda was the only British outpost to enjoy them. Thomas Pennant, in the 1760s, wrote, 'No bird is of such use to the islanders as this: the fulmar supplies them with oil for their lamps, down for their beds, a delicacy for their tables, a balm for their wounds, and a medicine for their distempers.' The St Kildans are said to have taken an annual toll of 12,000 fulmars, a half of the island production, as well as 2,000 adult gannets and 2,000 'gugas', their fat near-fledgling young. The birds were either clubbed or taken in a noose attached to the end of a long pole, then thrown out to fall in the sea below, where they were retrieved by men who stowed them in open boats. A high degree of courage was required, both in the cliff climbing and in the seamanship, to say nothing of the danger of being hit on the head by a dead guga weighing ten pounds (4·5 kg). Though the carnage may seem appalling to our late-twentieth-century sensitivities, this island community lived in natural harmony with the seabirds on their doorstep.

Left: Fulmar-hunting on St Kilda in the 1920s. A running noose at the end of a long pole is gently lowered over the head of a bird sitting on its nest.

Their lives were lived only by virtue of the existence of the seabirds but by all accounts they were satisfying lives, both culturally and physically. Human occupation of St Kilda dated from at least the fourteenth century till it succumbed to the corruptions and lure of advancing civilization in the twentieth.

Islanders in the Faeroes and Westmann Islands still take a yearly toll of their myriad seabirds but Sula Sgeir represents the only British gannetry from which young gannets may still be legally taken by the men of Lewis. If the cull is of young gannets, the effect on breeding numbers is small but the taking of adults does have an adverse effect unless there is a steady recruitment of breeding stock from other gannetries. With the species doing well at the moment, there is no shortage of willing recruits to Sula Sgeir.

In other parts of the world, the waste products of large seabirds, nesting in close proximity over a period of many thousands of years, have provided significant income to man. The phosphate- and nitrate-rich droppings on seabird islands off Peru are used in agriculture as a powerful fertilizer, marketed for hundreds of millions of pounds. The guanay cormorant, which gives its name to the product, guano, produces 35 lbs (16 kg) in a season; the cormorants breed in enormous numbers, along with brown pelicans and gannets (boobies). The ancient stocks of guano, accumulating since the Pleistocene epoch, were quarried out within a hundred years or so of their first exploitation by man, yet the industry is still sustained by the annual production. I do not think any serious use has been made of seabird excrement in Britain, presumably because the cost and difficulties of collection from such relatively small deposits makes the process unattractive.

On the other hand, birds' eggs have been enthusiastically harvested in Britain. Even in recent times of hardship, as in war, the eggs of gulls have made a useful addition to the national larder. In years past, the eggs of several gulls were collected in quantity. Black-headed gull colonies are conveniently set up inland among undemanding sand dunes and islands on lakes. Their nests were worked systematically at the beginning of the season and the harvesting ceased before the gulls became too discouraged to complete their clutches. As late as 1935, Leadenhall Market received 300,000 black-headed gull eggs.

Egg collecting on the coastal cliffs was a great deal less easy but 130,000 guillemot eggs were

Brown pelicans on the Ballestas Islands, Peru. Their mineral-rich droppings sustain a multi-million pound fertilizer industry.

taken from the cliffs at Bempton in 1884. Exploitation of these mainland sites developed on altogether too greedy a scale. The increase in human population, the more widespread availability and accuracy of firearms, coupled with vastly improved means of transport, reduced accessible seabird populations markedly. From about 1830, the boatmen of Bridlington and Scarborough became involved in a disreputable trade which devastated the Flamborough Head colonies. Chartered by parties of a few dozen 'gentlemen' at a time, they took their pleasure steamers to the foot of the cliffs, from which vantage point their clients let fly at the birds with shotguns. The result was a systematic destruction of the sitting auks and gulls. A contemporary correspondent wrote of two boats 'literally laden with birds, the boatmen sitting on them, and the birds heaped up in the bow and the stern above the gunwale'. This kind of mindless battue also went on at other seabird sites, for instance at the Bass Rock, the Isle of May, and on the islands of the Pembrokeshire coast but it was in the Yorkshire vicarage of Bridlington that dissenting opinion found its voice and an association for the protection of the birds was formed. Clergymen sent a letter to *The Times* newspaper, public opinion was stirred and a Sea Bird Act was passed in 1869.

Egg collecting on a more acceptable basis continued on the Bempton/Flamborough cliffs till about 1950. Nowadays, the collection of seabird eggs is a sporadic and disorganized affair, although the eggs are a natural resource that might well be better exploited. From a conservationist's point of view, well managed farming of a wild species may be the most effective way of ensuring the healthy continuance of a population. The excesses and disasters of the past occurred when birds were ruthlessly hunted without regard to biological principles.

Seabird protection on the Yorkshire cliffs had been preceded by a great deal of bird legislation, which, until that time, had been devoted to game species. In Britain, wild birds are not 'owned' by the landowner on whose land they find themselves, so a great deal of legal effort was devoted to establishing rights to wild gamebirds, endeavouring to make them the private property of the landowner. Until comparatively recently, most

Acts were aimed at safeguarding the landowner's rights; the object was only incidentally to preserve the game. Sporting rights have always been regarded as of great value and enlightened sportsmen themselves have been in the forefront of conservation legislation, since, of course, they have the strongest of incentives to see a continuing healthy population. It is also true that many sportsmen have been great champions of their prey in terms of aesthetic appreciation. The concept of animals as creatures to be shielded from the forces of predation and pressure is almost entirely a consequence of increasing urbanization and separation from rural roots of the human population.

The noblest of bird sports is falconry. Using birds of prey as hunting assistants dates back at least to the time of the Persians, in 1700 BC, and possibly to the early Chinese, in 2000 BC. The activity was at first a crude affair, in which beaters flushed small birds which were then attacked either by falcons in the air or by men with sticks if the birds feared to take wing. This form of hunting, in which birds of prey were taught to stoop on to a lure, a scrap of leather or material serving as imitation prey, before being 'entered' to the chosen quarry, eventually became refined to a highly formalized sport.

The terms used in falconry and the classification of bird species in relation to their human partners lent itself to a hierarchy. The birds themselves became status symbols. Gyrfalcons were reserved for royalty, peregrines for princes, dukes and earls (merlins for their wives), goshawks and sparrow-hawks for the gentry and the priests. The language of falconry further served to dignify the activity. Birds taken from the nest, or 'eyrie', are known as 'eyasses'. Those caught in their first plumage are 'passage hawks' and those in their second plumage 'haggards'. Female peregrines are 'falcons' to falconers, while the smaller males are 'tiercels'.

In training, the newly taken eyass is 'hacked' from a hacking post driven into a grassy lawn. Well-fed, it is encouraged to attack the lure, presented on the end of a long string and dragged over the grass. Because of the ever-present danger of losing a bird, the falconer only 'enters' it to quarry when it is 'sharp-set', or hungry. In this condition, he stands the greatest chance of recovering his falcon or hawk when offering the lure. Falcons and eagles were flown over the wide open spaces natural to the birds, while goshawks and sparrowhawks were worked over scrub and

Falconry, the sport of taking wild quarry with birds-of-prey, was perfected as an art form in the East. In the early Middle Ages it was the preserve of the aristocracy in Britain. The development of firearms caused it to decline in favour but a small band of dedicated enthusiasts keeps its noble traditions alive. This peregrine is rigged for the chase, with jesses and a bell on its legs. The hood serves to calm the bird and allows the falcon to be carried without fuss.

Cage-birds for sale at a street market in Salvador do Bahia, Brazil.

175

The Japanese and Chinese first fished with domesticated cormorants in the fifth century AD.

woodland. The sport was sociable and exciting. In the ninth century, the first of many laws was passed making falconry the special preserve of the nobility. Herons also became a protected species; protected, that is, for the enjoyment of royal sport.

Falconry flourished before the great open spaces of Britain became fenced and enclosed for farming. The ever-increasing sophistication of firearms persuaded most sportsmen and hunters to abandon the sport and today it retains only a pale shadow of its past glory. A small band of serious and dedicated enthusiasts runs the British Falconers Club, which aims to keep the ancient traditions alive. Unfortunately, there is a larger band of over-enthusiastic amateurs who bring the sport into disrepute. Birds of prey have faced centuries of persecution from keepers, egg-collectors and, more recently, poisonous chemicals. It seems hard that they have to face the inept methods and cruel captivity of these misguided 'falconers' who get a taste for the sport through seeing sentimental films in the cinema. Countless kestrels are stolen from their nests every year, to die forgotten in back yards.

I do not know whether ospreys have ever been trained to fish on behalf of a human owner but cormorants have served this purpose in Britain as well as in Japan, where the practice started. Like the falconer's birds, cormorants are trained for the job but, instead of being taken from the nest after hatching, they are taken as eggs and fostered by domestic fowls. The practice was apparently begun in the fifth century AD in Japan and subsequently spread to China. The birds wear soft leather collars which prevent them from swallowing the fish they catch. On returning to their handler's boat to release the catch, they are rewarded with pieces of fish or mashed beans. Cormorant fishing, which happens at night by the light of lanterns, is now largely a tourist attraction in Japan.

It is possible that the idea of cormorant fishing was brought back to Europe by Jesuit missionaries, because it seems that Louis XIII of France enjoyed the services of court cormorants at Fontainebleu in the early sixteenth century. By the time of James I, there was an official 'Master of the Cormorants' in England, a post still mentioned in 1661. In the mid-nineteenth century, the Rev. F. O. Morris wrote, 'I was invited once or twice the last few years by my friend Captain Arthur Brooksbank, of Middleton Hall, to go with him and Captain Salvin, to see the tame cormorants of the latter that fish in the Driffield streams below Wansford in my former parish of Nafferton, and was able on one of the occasions to accept the invitation. A sight well worth seeing it was.' It is a pity he does not say more but at least it shows that cormorant-hawking was alive and well in this country not so long ago.

Falconry and cormorant fishing are forms of domestication. Other birds lent themselves very much earlier to this relationship with man and their influence has proved more significant in that it has played a part in the remarkable spread and sucess of our own species. The beginnings of animal domestication probably date back to the Mesolithic age, when man developed weapons like the bow and arrow. Camp scavengers were probably easily persuaded to hang around for scraps and in this way man joined forces with dogs. By Neolithic times, farmers were already able to store enough food to sustain breeding stocks of cattle and goats through the winter. Doubtless, even then, they indulged in the enjoyable practice of bird-table feeding and it is likely that injured birds, tolerated as pets, might recover and remain to lay eggs or to be fattened for the pot.

Fowls have been pressed into service by man for thousands of years as religious sacrifices, for cock-fighting and as symbols of the waking day but most of all for food. Their parent stock were the jungle fowls of South East Asia. These birds enjoy a life style similar to any other of the pheasant family, laying a single clutch of eggs annually in a ground nest. Outside the breeding season, they are

Wild and domesticated fowl

Jungle fowl

Modern domestic fowl

Mallard

Aylesbury

Greylag

Embden goose

By selective breeding, we have made significant changes to the physical shape of wild fowls. The domestic chicken has more breast and leg muscle than the jungle version, but is less able to fend for itself. An Aylesbury may be four times as heavy as the wild mallard. The Embden goose is totally incapable of a gruelling migration flight.

sociable birds, working the forest edge and scrub country in flocks and roosting communally at night. Sociable behaviour like this is an important prerequisite for an animal likely to do well in domestication. Entertaining social relations with each other, they are more likely to take kindly to sharing life with another species.

The advantages and disadvantages of domestication are fairly evenly spread on both sides. From man's point of view, he gets greater return for less effort but the stock becomes less healthy and there is the constant problem of disease. From the animal's point of view, it gains protection and an easy supply of food but loses freedom of movement and must reproduce in a pattern which suits the master. Controlling the breeding process, man can physically change the animal to whatever extent its genetic potential allows. In the case of the jungle fowl, man was dealing with a highly malleable species, capable of great variation through selective breeding. Not only the bird's size but the distribution of muscle weight, plumage, egg-colour and even physiological traits are at his command.

The use of artificial incubators was well understood by the ancient Egyptians and Chinese poultry farmers at least 3,000 years ago. The Romans, who also used hens extensively to help them with prophesies, experimented with colour mutations and had a clear understanding of the economic aspects of poultry and egg production. Even the Celts in Britain had tasted chicken by the time the Romans arrived.

Left to fend for itself, the Asian jungle fowl will lay an egg a day till its clutch of half a dozen is complete. As is the case with many other species, it will continue laying if the eggs are taken from it until it achieves the visual stimulus of a full clutch. Continue stealing its eggs and it will continue laying. Egg potential varies from breed to breed but a modern purpose-bred hen can produce a staggering 340 eggs in her first year of production. In 1980, in Britain, forty-seven million laying pullets and hens turned out a gross egg production totalling more than thirteen thousand million. In the same year, 400 million birds were slaughtered for the table. The domestic fowl must be the commonest bird in the world.

All domestic ducks are descended from the wild mallard, which was probably first bred domestically in the Far East some 2,000 years ago. By Roman times, ducks were an important food source. Wild mallards will not breed in captivity,

Swans on the Thames at Eton (aquatint by William Daniell). Mute swans have been semi-domesticated for a thousand years, partly as a food source but also because they improve the scene.

so the eggs were collected from the wild and brooded by farmyard fowls. Even today, broody bantams are used when setting a clutch of duck eggs, as they make ideal foster mothers. Nowadays, there are a number of varieties of domestic duck, differing greatly in size, shape and function; some are for meat and some are for egg production, each the result of selective pressures applied by man. Many curious shapes and startling colours are also produced for 'the fancy'. The average wild mallard drake weighs 2½ lbs (1·1 kg), whereas the Aylesbury, which is the result of 1,000 years of selection, weighs 9 lbs (4 kg). Wild mallards lay a clutch of about ten eggs, only once in a season, but ducks bred for egg laying will behave like domestic fowls and lay almost daily through a great part of the year.

Domesticated forms of the wild greylag goose existed at least 4,000 years ago. By the time of

Homer, at least nine breeds were known. Their tendency to over-eat, given the opportunity, was fully utilized and birds were stuffed with soaked grain in order to make them fat and to discourage them from flying away. The Romans had good cause to venerate geese, which they regarded as highly intelligent, after they had saved Rome from sacking by the Gauls in 390 BC. The birds were kept in the temple of Juno, to whom they were sacred; when the invaders made their attack on the Capitol, they were foiled when the cackling birds raised the alarm.

The mute swan has been semi-domesticated in Britain since at least the tenth century. Nesting conspicuously on the banks of quiet waterways, it must always have been a simple matter to take cygnets from the nest to rear and fatten for the table. Early on, swans achieved unique status as 'Royal Birds', subject to the crown. If they escaped from private waters, they became 'estrays'; that is, 'any Beast that is not wild found within a lordship and not owned by any man'. Jacob's *Law Dictionary* of 1732 went on to explain that, in the case of an 'estray', 'if it be cried and proclaimed according to Law in the next two Market-Towns on two Market Days, and is not claimed by the owner within a Year and a Day, it belongs to the Lord of the Liberty. And swans may be estray, as well as Beasts, and are to be proclaimed'. The Crown could and often did grant the right to privileged subjects to keep swans on common waters, provided the birds were pinioned and marked.

The motive for keeping swans was partly for the food they represented and partly for the pleasure of seeing them on water but also, importantly, for the status they conferred, as birds of royal birth. At Abbotsbury, in Dorset, swans have been provided with nest sites and cared for by a swanherd for 600 years. At first, they belonged to the Benedictine Order of Monks at St Peter's Monastery but, after the Dissolution, Henry VIII granted the manor of Abbotsbury, together with the swannery rights, to the Fox-Strangways family, whose descendants, the heirs of the Earl of Ilchester, are still the owners. The number of swans is carefully controlled, so that the natural food resources of the Fleet (the extensive brackish lagoon inside the Chesil Beach) are maintained. Elsewhere in Britain and in most of northwest Europe, the population is increasing rapidly.

Swans are said to have been one of the traditional Christmas dishes, till the arrival of the turkey. While it is generally accepted that swans are British by nationality, in spite of a certain amount of controversy and the suggestion that they were introduced by the Romans, there is no question that turkeys are exotic foreigners. The turkey was domesticated by pre-conquest Indians in North America from a Mexican subspecies of the wild turkey, a forest bird, very early in that continent's history. It was brought back to England by the returning 'Conquistadores' in the early sixteenth century and soon found its way to Britain in about 1525.

Another bird was introduced by seafaring men at about the same time, though this one was destined for ornamental bird cages and less likely to end up in the kitchen. Originally, the canary, as brought from the Canary Isles, was not a strikingly beautiful bird but was prized for its song. Accelerated selection processes soon produced the more colourful birds we know today. Budgerigars, those other companions to the lonely, arrived more recently. They were brought from Australia by John Gould, the ornithologist

Melopsittacus undulatus, the budgerigar. A painting by John Gould from his *Birds of Australia*.
It was John Gould who first brought budgies to Britain in 1840.

and artist, in 1840. A highly sociable desert species, this green parakeet flocks at waterholes in countless numbers in the wild; there have been breeding colonies of more than a million birds. Now it is the world's most popular cage bird. From its natural green colour, it has been enthusiastically bred through yellows and blues to the multi-coloured birds we all know and many love. Easy to feed, eating mainly seeds, and affectionate in song, it has the magic ability to 'talk', which is its great selling feature.

Pigeons have been domesticated for possibly longer than any other bird and they are still much used by man in the fields of sport, science, companionship and, in some countries, food. In early Asian cultures, they were sacred birds, symbols of the love goddess Astarte, or Astoreth, whose worship was marked by uninhibited displays of licentiousness. Pigeons were popular in temples as symbols of love and fertility. Though the Old Testament saw them first as symbols of wickedness, Christianity finally took them under its wings and sanitized them into symbols of heavenly love, in which form they became more respectable. Western domestication proceeded apace, aided by the comfortable discovery that not only did the birds taste good but that they had certain other characteristics which made them highly desirable in economic terms.

The wild species which fathered these birds-for-all-seasons was the rock dove, which originated in the arid, treeless regions of the Mediterranean and points east. Rock doves need open country for foraging. As the Romans penetrated north, clearing forests and replacing them with fields and pasture, a sympathetic environment was created for the birds, whose distribution was accordingly extended. Where there are no trees, they make do with nest sites on ledges, on cliffs, in caves and in gorges. In Britain, they became a coastal species, breeding in caves and rocky fissures, foraging on rough cliff pastures and cultivated fields. They have the astonishing facility of raising anything up to ten families a year, two eggs at a time, sitting on fresh ones while the young of the previous brood are barely fledged.

It was this fecundity that so impressed man. On the Welsh and Scottish coasts, he 'improved' the sea caves by carving ledges and building pigeon-holes to encourage the rock doves to breed in places from which he could conveniently collect the fat squabs. Soon he realized that, using such tractable birds, he could set up semi-domesticated breeding colonies far from the sea. This was the beginning of an avicultural technique which flowered in the Middle Ages. The pigeon house, or dove-cote, often housed 500 pairs of pigeons, carefully husbanded and cropped by intensive rearing methods, with the over-riding advantage that the birds were free-flying and found their own food. However, not surprisingly, the right to keep pigeons was jealously guarded by the ruling classes and the peasants had to endure the sight of the Lord of the Manor's pigeons raiding their crops. This created considerable friction. Indeed, the depredations of pigeons was one of the contributory factors leading up to the French Revolution.

In the eighteenth century, farmers developed root crops, which made it possible for them to feed more than their basic breeding stock of cattle, sheep and pigs through the winter. The availability of more conventional meat during the hard winter days made the pigeon houses redundant and they fell into disuse.

Pigeons are adaptable birds, though, and they found homes elsewhere. Scientists used their phenomenal breeding rate in genetic experiments and studied their diversity of races. Darwin, for example, showed them to have descended from a single ancestral form and was thus stimulated to work on his evolutionary theory. 'Fanciers' used those same breeding propensities to select bizarre strains for 'show'. Generations of racing enthusiasts used them to power a sport which owes much to Darwin's enthusiastic research. Racing pigeons are superb specimens, sturdy stock, selected and line-bred for speed and endurance, then cross-bred for the desirable hybrid quality of vigour. Something like two million people maintain pigeon lofts and race pigeons for huge sums of money. Giant pigeon-transporters trundle down the motorways and across the Channel, carrying hundreds of crates with 3,000 or 4,000 birds, all desperate for release and a quick flight back to their waiting eggs.

Many of these racing pigeons drop out of their racing careers, to find a new life in city streets, joining the descendants of the rejected dove-cote pigeons in begging for scraps. Others stop off at the coast, reverting to the life-style of those far-off ancestors who all came from the wild coastal rock pigeon. Though the truly wild rock doves are rare nowadays, few suitable cliffs lack the lovely sight of a flock of birds with their characteristic two black wingbars taking a turn round the bay before

Pigeons were possibly the first birds to be domesticated; in early Asian cultures they were sacred symbols of the goddess of love, a tribute to their astonishing fertility. In Britain the coastal rock doves were first encouraged to breed on artificial cave-ledges, for the sake of their highly edible fat squabs. In the Middle Ages they were taken and established in dovecotes, which still stand in many parts of the country. For instance (*above*), the one at Dunster in Somerset. The birds flew free, to forage far and wide, returning to enter the dovecote by way of the 'lantern' at the top to nest in the pigeon-holes (*left*). The ladder is attached to a revolving stage and is an ingenious device which allows the pigeon-keeper easy access to every nest. Nowadays we no longer breed pigeons on this factory-farming system for food, but huge numbers are selectively bred by racing enthusiasts. Something like two million people maintain pigeon lofts and race pigeons for money. Giant transporters convey the birds to release points all over Britain and the Continent.

Right, above: A typical release.

Right, below: The birds carry an identifying numbered ring on their legs, but may also be rubber-stamped with a home address on their primary flight feathers.

Above: Eiders breed mainly in Iceland and Scandinavia, but their increasing range includes the coasts of northern Britain. To keep the eggs warm when the duck leaves the nest temporarily, the lining is of her warm breast feathers—eiderdown. Eiders like to nest *by* something an old fish box serving very well. The eiderdown farmers take advantage of this trait by providing suitable stones to encourage the birds to nest in close company, so facilitating the collection of feathers.

Left: Pigeons outside their nest holes above the promenade, Goodrington, Devon. Racing pigeons often drop out and choose to live a life of leisured ease at the seaside, thus reverting to the lifestyle of their original rock dove stock.

flying in to their secret crevices and their squabs. While the peregrine is still relatively rare, they have little to worry about.

As well as providing fat squabs, pigeons also provided a useful bonus to continental farmers in the rich fertilizer of their droppings; the pile of guano which accumulated on the floors of pigeon houses was carefully collected and used to feed the grape vines. In addition, the soft down feathers of the squabs were probably put to good use in mattresses and pillows but the prime sources of top quality insulating feathers for domestic use have always been geese and ducks; the most valuable feathers come from the eider duck of eiderdown fame.

Eiders come from the Arctic, breeding extensively in Iceland and Scandinavia but reaching down to northern Britain and the Low Countries and steadily expanding their range southwards. They are one of the most numerous ducks in the world, with a winter population in Europe alone of more than two million. Handsome black and white birds, with a strikingly wedge-shaped beak and head, they are coastal sea-ducks, nesting just behind the shores of sea lakes and islands, never very far from the water. The nest site is just a small hollow, usually in the lee of a rock or a clump of vegetation, lined with a few bits of grass or anything that is available, then finished with a lining of down feathers which the duck pulls from her own breast. This lining is quite substantial; if the duck leaves the nest for a while, she arranges an eiderdown quilt over the eggs to cover and keep them warm.

The warmth-retaining qualities of the eider's down have generated a healthy market for the feathers and, especially in Iceland, the birds are encouraged to nest by farmers who subsequently collect the nest lining. Eiders are strongly colonial; wild colonies contain as many as 3,000 pairs but farmers have managed to increase their well-protected colonies to as many as 5,000 pairs by the systematic provision of suitable nesting places. They do not need to construct special nest boxes. All they need to do is to set out a row of stones or sticks at the right distance apart (eiders will nest in close proximity at a density of two nests to not much more than a square yard). The ducks like to nest up against something, so they commandeer the marks provided. The eiderdown farms are protected with care. Their owners go to great lengths to make sure the season is successful; they even provide musical instruments to sound in the wind, though it is not clear just how conducive to success this really is.

Farmers also set up coloured ribbons on strings, another ruse which is supposed to please the ducks. In visiting the colony, where the birds are very tame, the farmers take great care to wear the same clothes every time and to follow the same strict route in walking. From the eiders' point of view, they have nothing to lose except their down feathers and, of course, these are not taken until they have served their natural purpose. The down is first collected just before the eggs hatch, when the top quality inner lining is removed from the nest. The less clean and tangled outer lining is taken after the young have left the nest. The sacks of down are sent to a central cleaning place for hand-sorting and marketing. The result is a substantial income for the eider farmers and increased breeding success for the eiders, a highly satisfactory co-operative venture. Not surprisingly, the eiders are strictly protected by law in Iceland and Denmark.

Bird feathers have been useful to man in many other ways. We may no longer use quills for pens but feathers still serve on the archer's arrows and on shuttlecocks. Fishermen use brightly coloured neck feathers and display feathers in tying their artificial flies. In Greenland, the skins of great northern divers are used for ornamental blankets and, in Europe, the elaborate display plumage of the great crested grebe was once popular in the clothing trade. The breast pelts, known as 'grebe fur', were used in the manufacture of hats, coats and muffs for women anxious to court high fashion. (A far cry from the St Kildan's use of gannet skins for shoes!) Little egrets have been farmed on a small scale for their plumes but in the past whole populations of herons have been wiped out in uncontrolled greed for profit.

Towards the end of the nineteenth century, the international fashion trade in bird plumage was getting out of hand and rousing great indignation. Fashion required hats, bonnets and dresses bedecked with stuffed birds. Twelve birds were stuffed to create one hat. A ball dress was covered completely with canary skins. ('I am glad to say the wearer of it, though handsome, had no partner,' commented one social critic.) London fashion houses started a run on the kingfishers of the Thames, using their brilliant feathers to decorate the women of society. Many people found the practice cruel and contemptible. The Rev. F. O. Morris, supported by the obligatory member of the aristocracy, Lady Mount-Temple, established the Plumage League in 1885. Its members, restricted to the female sex, sought to discourage the use of birds for adornment and suggested artificial plumage, in line with the use of artificial flowers.

Francis Morris had already had some success in marshalling public opinion; his was one of the guiding hands which had steered the Act for the Preservation of Seabirds through Parliament in 1869. And, when gaping loopholes were revealed in that Act, he had pressed for the enactment of the 1880 Wild Birds Protection Act, which established the principle of close seasons for wild birds, while nevertheless respecting landowners' rights. Morris knew how to mobilize the troops and he was a prolific letter writer with the magic touch for getting his work into the correspondence columns of *The Times*. He was working with a rising tide. In 1889, only four years after his exploratory Plumage League was started, yet another group of concerned women were giving birth to an organization which was destined to become a major force in conservation, The Royal Society for the Protection of Birds.

The initial motivation of the members was simply to stop the traffic in exotic bird plumage from egrets and birds of paradise destined for the millinery trade. Their objective was finally

Birds in fashion, nineteenth century. At one time Clovelly, in Devon, was the centre of a cottage industry, preparing large numbers of juvenile kittiwake wings for the millinery trade.

A delicately spread corpse decorates the 'Diaz chapeau' on the cover page of *Myra's Journal*, April 1882.

achieved in 1921, by which time public awareness of the aesthetic value of birds was already running far ahead of the ability of lawyers to draft effective Bills. Protection law is difficult to frame, since there are so many conflicting human interests, to say nothing of the different life styles of the creatures involved and the difficulty of deciding which are the 'goodies' and which the 'baddies' and precisely when and to what extent they are being good or bad. By 1939, there were sixteen separate Acts of Parliament involving bird protection.

In 1952, not a moment too soon (Morris had suggested it in 1868), the concept of protection for *all* birds, their nests and eggs was introduced, with exceptions scheduled as necessary in the interests of science, agriculture and sport. The Bill was more flexible and more effective than anything that had gone before (though it seemed to many that it went too far in branding egg-collecting boys as criminals, especially when almost every adult ornithologist or birdwatcher in the country had begun his interest with that activity) but there were

still many problems. An effective way of destroying birds is to destroy their habitat, yet the painstakingly-established concept of Sites of Special Scientific Interest (SSSIs), which often related to bird-rich places, still remained in 1980 as a pious ideal which landowners could flout without penalty. The painful process of refining the law began again in 1981, with the Wildlife and Countryside Bill, which represents the most recent but undoubtedly not the last word on official conservation policy.

Birds will flourish best, giving us best value in both economic and aesthetic fields, when everyone has a broad understanding of their vital place in our planet's ecology. For our own sakes, we need to manage Britain so that there is room for us to express a full life, birds and all. The enlightened mid-Victorians pursued the goal of preservation; those concerned today like to think that conservation offers a more healthy and positive management plan. Only time will tell but at least an enormous number of people do now care about birds.

187

EXPLOITATION OF BIRDS

Kestrel 'winnowing' over vole-rich land. Only slowly are people becoming aware that the relationship between the predator and its prey is healthy and mutually beneficial.

9
Tools
of the
Birdwatcher

Starting young.

You must be able to identify the birds you see. Of course, it would be perfectly possible to enjoy birds and birdsong without the faintest idea of their names but there would be a real problem every time you wanted to discuss them or convey your experiences to someone else. The best way of learning is to have a knowledgeable naturalist to take you by the hand and impart his information direct, in the field. Field trips with local societies may go some way to fulfilling this need but almost certainly you will have to work some of your birds out for yourself and for this a book is essential.

There are several good field guides on the market. The one you choose will depend on your preferences in the small differences between them. David Saunders's *RSPB Guide to British Birds*, published by Hamlyn, was written to help beginners find their way round the birds they are most likely to see and it makes an excellent first guide. Inevitably, you will want a more comprehensive coverage in due course and then you will move up to one of the big three guides, which provide material on a wider, European, basis, and which are more comprehensive in scope. The first is Peterson, Mountfort and Hollom's *Field Guide to the Birds of Britain and Europe*, first published by Collins in 1954 but having the advantage of innumerable revisions; the current edition is completely up-to-date and thoroughly reliable. Although the layout determines that the information and pictures are on separate pages and although the pagination is eccentric, the book nevertheless is a goldmine of succinct, reliable, well-marshalled information and I, for one, would never be without it. It is also a pleasure to handle and to browse through.

The second major field guide is also published by Collins but in this case they have improved the layout so that the pictures and text are married up more comfortably. Richard Fitter and John Parslow's *The Birds of Britain and Europe, North Africa and the Middle East* covers a wider geographical area than the Peterson guide and this has obvious advantages but inevitably the increased number of species included make for confusion for the beginner who is primarily concerned with the United Kingdom and the neighbouring continent.

Lastly, *The Hamlyn Guide to the Birds of Britain and Europe*, written by Bertel Bruun is well laid out and gives basic information on 516 species; it covers a more than adequate area and is easy to use. The fact is that all three of these guides are

admirable but I would suggest that the Peterson or the Bruun are most suitable for a newcomer. To your basic field guide add a copy of P. A. D. Hollom's *The Popular Handbook of British Birds*, published by H. F. & G. Witherby, and you have the nucleus of a bird library, though I warn you that there will be no end to the number of bird books you will want to own. The most authoritative and comprehensive reference work on the ornithology of our region is currently being issued by the Oxford University Press in seven parts: three volumes have so far been published of *The Handbook of the Birds of Europe, the Middle East and North Africa (The Birds of the Western Palearctic)*.

While you are almost certainly going to carry your field guide with you on birding trips, it is most important to have a good look at your quarry and to digest as much as you can about it before rushing to the picture pages for an identification. In much the same way as you contract instant diseases as you read a book of home medicine, it is very easy to transform your garden birds into the most exotic visitors when you start searching the pages. Your most valuable tools are your own senses, especially eyes and ears, and your impressions and observations should be crystallized and committed to paper *before* you consult the guide, if you want to take the job seriously. So a notebook and pencil are vital pieces of equipment. Note the arrival and departure dates of seasonal visitors, along with bare details of weather and location. Note time, date, place, habitat, grid reference, size (by comparison with other birds), colour of plumage, shape of body, bill, legs, posture, behaviour, calls or song. Is the bird alone or in company? What is it doing, or eating? How does it move, fly? Photographs and tapes may be useful but far and away the most important thing is to look and listen carefully. Make a rough sketch of the bird, if you like, to help you to remember its notable features. Field sketches can sometimes become a useful permanent record.

When you are good at looking at birds, you might see 100 species in a day. Without leaving Europe, you might amass a life list of more than 400 species. But the numbers game is not everything and most people get most pleasure out of their everyday garden birds where the total maximum of species is probably not more than forty.

You must have the best pair of binoculars that

you can afford but choosing the right pair for your purposes is far from easy. (If you are rich there is a lot of sense in owning a half a dozen different pairs, chosen for different jobs on different days in different places!) Avoid heavy glasses if you are going to be walking a great deal with them. Avoid high magnification like the plague unless it is coupled with exceptional light-gathering power and you are going to mount the instrument on a tripod. The zoom binoculars which appear such a perfect solution to these problems are mostly a mistake, because they are heavy and the optical quality is less than excellent. On the whole, it is best to avoid gimmicks and special offers. Stick to the advertisement pages of *Birds* and *British Birds* and you will not go far wrong. The RSPB now market their own glasses under the *Avocet* trademark and these are good value at the cheaper end of the range.

Binoculars are described in a combination of two figures; for instance, 8 × 30. The first figure indicates the magnification involved and the second indicates the diameter in millimetres of the object lenses. Do not make the assumption that you should plump for the highest magnification

Birdwatching in the grand manner. The RSPB's achievements at Minsmere were celebrated in a series of live transmissions on BBC 2 during one day in June, 1981. Cameras set up in the hides showed a glimpse of the rich birdlife to some ten million viewers. The *Birdwatch* circus included a mobile canteen, generators, control and radiolink vans, yet the birds on the other side of the sea-wall were unaware of its existence!

Jeremy Sorensen, the RSPB's warden at Minsmere, in the commentator's hide with Tony Soper.

available. I use a pair of 7× glasses mostly and their magnification is more than adequate for most purposes. Coupled with a light gathering power of 50 (i.e. they are described as 7×50 glasses), they give a high quality, bright picture, even in poorly lit conditions. It is important to remember that a great deal of your birdwatching will be done early or late in the day or in dimly lit woodland edge. Because the relatively low magnification means that the binoculars can be held steadily even on a moving boat, 7×50 is the more or less standard size for marine use. The disadvantage of this size is that it is generally heavy.

Glasses of 8×30, 9×35 or 40, with centre focusing, represent general purpose instruments, giving good results with light weight. If you are dealing with distant subjects, then you may well end up with a pair of 10×50 or even 12×50, though the latter will have to be in steady hands if you are not going to endure a shaky picture and their field of view (their angle) is progressively reduced. Beyond a magnification of 12×, you are entering a realm where few experienced birdwatchers would follow you. Unfortunately, the larger sizes often figure in the sale pages of magazines, glowingly described in terms of high magnification but with little reference to the necessity for tripods built like battleships and arclights to provide illumination. For distant spotting of birds far out on a reservoir, for instance, you may find a telescope useful. Reputable models have zoom lenses working from 20 to 60×, so that you may locate your subject at the widest angle before zooming in on it. Telescopes are not much use for birdwatching at or on the sea, where there is usually a great deal too much movement for comfort, in more ways than one!

Perhaps the best plan is to buy an honest pair of *Avocet* glasses from the RSPB and to use them for a year or two till you decide on a long-term purchase, borrowing as many different models as you can during your trial period whenever you get the chance. There is an excellent pamphlet on *Binoculars and telescopes* published by the British Trust for Ornithology, Beech Grove, Tring, Herts.

Long before you have chosen your dream binoculars and are well on the way to your life-list of 400 plus, you will have felt the need to join one of the national bird organizations, in order to add your weight to the conservation movement and to benefit from the exchange of information and views in their magazines. Here is a guide to the main societies.

Royal Society for the Protection of Birds
The Lodge,
Sandy,
Bedfordshire,
SG19 2DL.

The largest voluntary conservation organization in Europe, with more than 450,000 members. The RSPB was founded in 1889 and has grown in stature with the years. It exists to promote the interests of birds but in fulfilling its task it effectively acts for the benefit of all Classes of animals in that it manages reserves in order to produce a diversity of life-forms. It may well encourage worms because they are eaten by blackbirds but the long term result is good for worms too! As well as setting up reserves, the RSPB is active in the fields of legislation and education. Regional offices and local representatives serve all areas and there are a number of local members centres. First class magazine, *Birds*. Junior section, the Young Ornithologists' Club. Publishes a number of useful leaflets, for those who want guidance on such things as: *The Birdwatcher's Code of Conduct* (see page 196), *Wild Birds and the Law, Information on Oil Pollution, Information on Effects of Pesticides, Information on Birds and the Law, Treatment of Sick, Orphaned and Injured Birds.*

British Trust for Ornithology
Beech Grove,
Tring,
Hertfordshire,
HP23 5NR.

Co-ordinates and leads the work of amateur ornithologists. Maintains a headquarters staff of professional biologists, whose object is to advance our understanding of the part birds play in our ecosystem. Much of its work is government funded. Organizes long-running survey and census work, administrates the bird-ringing scheme and collates the results. The Common Bird Census is a massive field operation which gathers data on bird numbers and distribution and analyses the natural and man-induced causes of change and fluctuation in the overall bird picture. This enquiry has provided invaluable information on the effect on our environment of changes in forestry and agricultural practices. The long-term aim is to produce an avian Domesday Book. The Nest Records Scheme amasses data on the breeding performance of British birds, in matters such as seasonal timing, clutch size and fledgling success. In these endeavours, as in other work such as the Garden Bird Feeding Survey, serious and conscientious amateurs are welcomed and encouraged. Quarterly journal, *Bird Study*.

Apart from offering food on a bird table and growing a bird garden full of berry-bearing shrubs and insect-rich borders, one of the best ways of attracting birds is by erecting nest-boxes. This is the RSPB's enclosed type, with blue tits the most likely customers. (Catalogue from RSPB, Sandy, Beds.)

British Ornithologists' Union
c/o The Zoological Society of London, Regent's Park, London NW1 4RY.

The major academic society, founded in 1858 by Professor Alfred Newton. Object to 'advance the science of Ornithology'. Membership by election. Publishes the leading ornithological journal, *Ibis*. Encourages and sponsors research, in liaison with the RSPB and BTO.

County and local bird groups are easily located through your local Public Library. The Army, Navy and Air Force all run birdwatching societies.

Bird courses, amongst other subjects, are run by the Field Studies Council, Preston Montford, Montford Bridge, Shrewsbury, Shropshire SY4 1HW, at their centres all over England and Wales. In Scotland, the Scottish Ornithologists Club, 21 Regent Terrace, Edinburgh EH7 5BT could possibly advise on field courses.

An invaluable guide to just about every activity, address, observatory, fieldwork project and assorted odds and ends will be found in *The Birdwatchers Yearbook*, published annually by the Buckingham Press, Rostherne, Hall Close, Maids Moreton, Buckingham MK18 1RH.

The main, and indispensable, bird magazine is the monthly *British Birds*, which publishes original material dealing with the birds of the western palearctic. Apart from major papers, it includes fascinating notes, reviews, the best of bird photography and enlivens the whole with personality pieces and competitions of a mildly academic nature. Subscription details or a free sample copy from Mrs Erika Sharrock, Fountains, Park Lane, Blunham, Bedford MK44 3NJ.

A useful book for those wanting to know more about injured birds is A. E. Cooper and J. T. Galey's *First Aid and Care of Wild Birds*, published by David and Charles, 1979.

If you want some guidance on cameras and sound recording equipment, two good books are J. Marchington and A. Clay's *Introduction to Bird and Wildlife Photography* and R. Margoschis's *Recording Natural History Sounds*.

The Birdwatcher's Code of Conduct

The Ten Commandments

1. **The welfare of birds must come first.**
2. **Habitat must be protected.**
3. **Keep disturbance to birds and their habitat to a minimum.**
4. **When you find a rare bird think carefully about whom you should tell.**
5. **Do not harass rare migrants.**
6. **Abide by the Bird Protection Acts at all times.**
7. **Respect the rights of landowners.**
8. **Respect the rights of other people in the countryside.**
9. **Make your records available to the local bird recorder.**
10. **Behave abroad as you would when bird-watching at home.**

1. Welfare of birds must come first

Whether your particular interest is photography, ringing, sound recording, scientific study or just birdwatching, remember that the welfare of the bird must always come first.

2. Habitat protection

Its habitat is vital to a bird and therefore we must ensure that our activities do not cause damage.

3. Keep disturbance to a minimum

Birds' tolerance of disturbance varies between species and seasons. Therefore, it is safer to keep all disturbance to a minimum. No birds should be disturbed from the nest in case opportunities for predators to take eggs or young are increased. In very cold weather disturbance to birds may cause them to use vital energy at a time when food is difficult to find. Wildfowlers already impose bans during cold weather: birdwatchers should exercise similar discretion.

4. Rare breeding birds

If you discover a rare bird breeding and feel that protection is necessary, inform the appropriate RSPB Regional Office, or the Species Protect-ion Department at the Lodge. Otherwise it is best in almost all circumstances to keep the record strictly secret in order to avoid disturbance by other birdwatchers and attacks by egg-collectors. Never visit known sites of rare breeding birds unless they are adequately protected. Even your presence may give away the site to others and cause so many other visitors that the birds may fail to breed successfully.

Disturbance at or near the nest of species

Telescopes can be very useful when watching birds at great distances, as on lakes or reservoirs, but they need to be supported on tripods.

listed on the First Schedule of the Protection of Birds Act, 1954, is a criminal offence.

Copies of *Wild Birds and the Law* are obtainable from the RSPB, The Lodge, Sandy, Beds SG19 2DL.

5. Rare migrants

Rare migrants or vagrants must not be harassed. If you discover one, consider the circumstances carefully before telling anyone. Will an influx of birdwatchers disturb the bird or others in the area? Will the habitat be damaged? Will problems be caused with the landowner?

6. Protection of Birds Acts

The bird protection laws are the result of hard campaigning by previous generations of birdwatchers. As birdwatchers we must abide by them at all times and not allow them to fall into disrepute.

7. Respect the rights of landowners

The wishes of landowners and occupiers of land must be respected. Do not enter land without permission. Comply with permit schemes. If you are leading a group, do give advance notice of the visit, even if a formal permit scheme is not in operation. Always obey the Country Code.

8. Respect the rights of other people

Have proper consideration for other birdwatchers. Try not to disrupt their activities or scare the birds they are watching. There are many other people who also use the countryside. Do not interfere with their activities and, if it seems that what they are doing is causing unnecessary disturbance to birds, do try to take a balanced view. Flushing gulls when walking a dog on a beach may do little harm, while the same dog might be a serious disturbance at a tern colony. When pointing this out to a non-birdwatcher be courteous, but firm. The non-birdwatchers' goodwill towards birds must not be destroyed by the attitudes of birdwatchers.

9. Keeping records

Much of today's knowledge about birds is the result of meticulous record keeping by our predecessors. Make sure you help to add to tomorrow's knowledge by sending records to your county bird recorder.

10. Birdwatching abroad

Behave abroad as you would at home. This code should be firmly adhered to when abroad (whatever the local laws). Well behaved birdwatchers can be important ambassadors for bird protection.

This code was drafted after consultation between the British Ornithologists' Union, British Trust for Ornithology, the Royal Society for the Protection of Birds, the Scottish Ornithologists' Club, the Wildfowl Trust and the Editors of *British Birds*.

List of British and Irish Birds

(originally published by the independent monthly journal British Birds*)*

1. This list follows the sequence and scientific nomenclature of Professor Dr K. H. Voous (1977, List of Recent Holarctic Bird Species).

2. The letters in the left hand column are defined as follows . . .

A. Species which have been recorded in an apparently wild state in Britain or Ireland at least once within the last 50 years.

B. Species which have been recorded in an apparently wild state in Britain or Ireland at least once but not within the last 50 years.

C. Species which, although originally introduced by man, have now established a regular feral breeding stock which apparently maintains itself without necessary recourse to further introduction.

D. Species which have been recorded within the last 50 years and would otherwise appear in category A except that: (i) there is a reasonable doubt that they have ever occurred in a wild state or (ii) they have certainly arrived with ship assistance or (iii) they have only ever been found dead on the tideline; also species which would otherwise appear in category C except that their feral populations may or may not be self-supporting.

3. The letters in the centre column are classified as follows . . .

R. Resident, or present at all seasons in comparable numbers.

S. Summer visitor, present in significantly greater numbers in summer than at other seasons.

W. Winter visitor, present in significantly greater numbers in winter than at other seasons.

P. Passage migrant, occurring in greater numbers on migration in spring and/or autumn than in summer or winter.

V. Vagrant, occurring so rarely that all records are listed annually in the report by the British Birds Rarities Committee (which requires written descriptions to substantiate sightings).

4. The number in the third column provides an indication of the number of pairs breeding, or having bred, in Britain and Ireland.

0 has bred, but does not now breed regularly.
1 1–10 pairs
2 11–100 pairs
3 101–1,000 pairs
4 1,001–10,000 pairs
5 10,001–100,000 pairs
6 100,001–1 million pairs
7 more than 1 million pairs

Non-passeriformes

GAVIIDAE

A	R	3	Red-throated Diver *Gavia stellata*
A	R	3	Black-throated Diver *G. arctica*
A	W	0	Great Northern Diver *G. immer*
A	V	.	White-billed Diver *G. adamsii*

PODICIPEDIDAE

A	V	.	Pied-billed Grebe *Podilymbus podiceps*
A	R	5	Little Grebe *Tachybaptus ruficollis*
A	R	4	Great Crested Grebe *Podiceps cristatus*
A	W	.	Red-necked Grebe *P. grisegena*
A	W	2	Slavonian Grebe *P. auritus*
A	W	2	Black-necked Grebe *P. nigricollis*

DIOMEDEIDAE

A	V	.	Black-browed Albatross *Diomedea melanophris*

PROCELLARIIDAE

A	R	6	Fulmar *Fulmarus glacialis*
B	V	.	Capped Petrel *Pterodroma hasitata*
A	V	.	Bulwer's Petrel *Bulweria bulwerii*
A	V	.	Cory's Shearwater *Calonectris diomedea*
A	P	.	Great Shearwater *Puffinus gravis*
A	P	.	Sooty Shearwater *P. griseus*
A	S	6	Manx Shearwater *P. puffinus*
A	V	.	Little Shearwater *P. assimilis*

HYDROBATIDAE

A	V	.	Wilson's Petrel *Oceanites oceanicus*
B	V	.	White-faced Petrel *Pelagodroma marina*
A	R	6	Storm Petrel *Hydrobates pelagicus*
A	P	4	Leach's Petrel *Oceanodroma leucorhoa*
A	V	.	Madeiran Petrel *O. castro*

SULIDAE

A	R	6	Gannet *Sula bassana*

PHALACROCORACIDAE

A	R	4	Cormorant *Phalacrocorax carbo*
A	R	5	Shag *P. aristotelis*

PELECANIDAE
D V . White Pelican *Pelecanus onocrotalus*

FREGATIDAE
A V . Magnificent Frigatebird *Fregata magnificens*

ARDEIDAE
A R 2 Bittern *Botaurus stellaris*
A V . American Bittern *B. lentiginosus*
A V . Little Bittern *Ixobrychus minutus*
A V . Night Heron *Nycticorax nycticorax*
B V . Green Heron *Butorides striatus*
A V . Squacco Heron *Ardeola ralloides*
A V . Cattle Egret *Bubulcus ibis*
A V . Little Egret *Egretta garzetta*
A V . Great White Egret *E. alba*
A R 4 Grey Heron *Ardea cinerea*
A V . Purple Heron *A. purpurea*

CICONIIDAE
A V . Black Stork *Ciconia nigra*
A V 0 White Stork *C. ciconia*

THRESKIORNITHIDAE
A V . Glossy Ibis *Plegadis falcinellus*
A P . Spoonbill *Platalea leucorodia*

PHOENICOPTERIDAE
D V . Greater Flamingo *Phoenicopterus ruber*

ANATIDAE
A R 4 Mute Swan *Cygnus olor*
A W . Bewick's Swan *C. columbianus*
A W 0 Whooper Swan *C. cygnus*
A W . Bean Goose *Anser fabalis*
A W . Pink-footed Goose *A. brachyrhynchus*
A W . White-fronted Goose *A. albifrons*
A V . Lesser White-fronted Goose *A. erythropus*
A R 3 Greylag Goose *A. anser*
A W . Snow Goose *A. caerulescens*
A R 4 Canada Goose *Branta canadensis*
A W . Barnacle Goose *B. leucopsis*
A W . Brent Goose *B. bernicla*
A V . Red-breasted Goose *B. ruficollis*
C R 3 Egyptian Goose *Alopochen aegyptiacus*
A V . Ruddy Shelduck *Tadorna ferruginea*
A R 5 Shelduck *T. tadorna*
D R 2 Wood Duck *Aix sponsa*
C R 3 Mandarin *A. galericulata*
A W 3 Wigeon *Anas penelope*
A V . American Wigeon *A. americana*
P V . Falcated Duck *A. falcata*
A R 3 Gadwall *A. strepera*
D V . Baikal Teal *A. formosa*
A R 4 Teal *A. crecca*
A R 6 Mallard *A. platyrhynchos*
A V . Black Duck *A. rubripes*
A W 2 Pintail *A. acuta*

A P 2 Garganey *A. querquedula*
A V . Blue-winged Teal *A. discors*
A R 3 Shoveler *A. clypeata*
A P 1 Red-crested Pochard *Netta rufina*
A W 3 Pochard *Aythya ferina*
A V . Ring-necked Duck *A. collaris*
A W . Ferruginous Duck *A. nyroca*
A W 4 Tufted Duck *A. fuligula*
A W 0 Scaup *A. marila*
A R 5 Eider *Somateria mollissima*
A V . King Eider *S. spectabilis*
A V . Steller's Eider *Polysticta stelleri*
A V . Harlequin Duck *Histrionicus histrionicus*
A W . Long-tailed Duck *Clangula hyemalis*
A P 3 Common Scoter *Melanitta nigra*
A V . Surf Scoter *M. perspicillata*
A W . Velvet Scoter *M. fusca*
A V . Bufflehead *Bucephala albeola*
A W 1 Goldeneye *B. clangula*
A V . Hooded Merganser *Mergus cucullatus*
A W . Smew *M. albellus*
A R 4 Red-breasted Merganser *M. serrator*
A R 4 Goosander *M. merganser*
C R 2 Ruddy Duck *Oxyura jamaicensis*

ACCIPITRIDAE
A P 2 Honey Buzzard *Pernis apivorus*
A V . Black Kite *Milvus migrans*
A R 2 Red Kite *M. milvus*
A V 0 White-tailed Eagle *Haliaeetus albicilla*
B V . Egyptian Vulture *Neophron percnopterus*
B V . Griffon Vulture *Gyps fulvus*
A P 1 Marsh Harrier *Circus aeruginosus*
A R 3 Hen Harrier *C. cyaneus*
A V . Pallid Harrier *C. macrourus*
A P 1 Montagu's Harrier *C. pygargus*
A R 2 Goshawk *Accipiter gentilis*
A R 5 Sparrowhawk *A. nisus*
A R 4 Buzzard *Buteo buteo*
A P . Rough-legged Buzzard *B. lagopus*
B V . Spotted Eagle *Aquila clanga*
A R 3 Golden Eagle *A. chrysaetos*

PANDIONIDAE
A P 2 Osprey *Pandion haliaetus*

FALCONIDAE
A V . Lesser Kestrel *Falco naumanni*
A R 6 Kestrel *F. tinnunculus*
A V . American Kestrel *F. sparverius*
A V . Red-footed Falcon *F. vespertinus*
A R 3 Merlin *F. columbarius*
A S 3 Hobby *F. subbuteo*
P V . Eleonora's Falcon *F. eleonorae*
P V . Saker *F. cherrug*
A V . Gyrfalcon *F. rusticolus*
A R 3 Peregrine *F. peregrinus*

TETRAONIDAE

A R 6 Willow/Red Grouse *Lagopus lagopus*
A R 5 Ptarmigan *L. mutus*
A R 5 Black Grouse *Tetrao tetrix*
C R 4 Capercaillie *T. urogallus*

PHASIANIDAE

D R 2 Bobwhite *Colinus virginianus*
C R 6 Red-legged Partridge *Alectoris rufa*
A R 6 Grey Partridge *Perdix perdix*
A S 3 Quail *Coturnix coturnix*
D R 2 Reeves's Pheasant *Syrmaticus reevesii*
C R 6 Pheasant *Phasianus colchicus*
C R 3 Golden Pheasant *Chrysolophus pictus*
C R 3 Lady Amherst's Pheasant *C. amherstiae*

RALLIDAE

A W 4 Water Rail *Rallus aquaticus*
A P 1 Spotted Crake *Porzana porzana*
A V . Sora Rail *P. carolina*
A V . Little Crake *P. parva*
A V 0 Baillon's Crake *P. pusilla*
A S 4 Corncrake *Crex crex*
A R 6 Moorhen *Gallinula chloropus*
B V . Allen's Gallinule *Porphyrula alleni*
A V . American Purple Gallinule *P. martinica*
A R 5 Coot *Fulica atra*

GRUIDAE

A V 0 Crane *Grus grus*
B V . Sandhill Crane *G. canadensis*

OTIDIDAE

A V . Little Bustard *Tetrax tetrax*
A V . Houbara Bustard *Chlamydotis undulata*
A V 0 Great Bustard *Otis tarda*

HAEMATOPODIDAE

A R 5 Oystercatcher *Haematopus ostralegus*

RECURVIROSTRIDAE

A V 0 Black-winged Stilt *Himantopus himantopus*
A R 3 Avocet *Recurvirostra avosetta*

BURHINIDAE

A R 3 Stone-curlew *Burhinus oedicnemus*

GLAREOLIDAE

A V . Cream-coloured Courser *Cursorius cursor*
A V . Collared Pratincole *Glareola pratincola*
A V . Black-winged Pratincole *G. nordmanni*

CHARADRIIDAE

A S 3 Little Ringed Plover *Charadrius dubius*
A R 4 Ringed Plover *C. hiaticula*
A V . Killdeer *C. vociferus*
A P 0 Kentish Plover *C. alexandrinus*
B V . Caspian Plover *C. asiaticus*
A S 2 Dotterel *C. morinellus*

A V . Lesser Golden Plover *Pluvialis dominica*
A R 5 Golden Plover *P. apricaria*
A W . Grey Plover *P. squatarola*
A V . Sociable Plover *Chettusia gregaria*
A V . White-tailed Plover *C. leucura*
A R 6 Lapwing *Vanellus vanellus*

SCOLOPACIDAE

A W . Knot *Calidris canutus*
A W . Sanderling *C. alba*
A V . Semipalmated Sandpiper *C. pusilla*
A V . Western Sandpiper *C. mauri*
A P . Little Stint *C. minuta*
A P 1 Temminck's Stint *C. temminckii*
A V . Least Sandpiper *C. minutilla*
A V . White-rumped Sandpiper *C. fuscicollis*
A V . Baird's Sandpiper *C. bairdii*
A P . Pectoral Sandpiper *C. melanotos*
A V . Sharp-tailed Sandpiper *C. acuminata*
A P . Curlew Sandpiper *C. ferruginea*
A W . Purple Sandpiper *C. maritima*
A W 4 Dunlin *C. alpina*
A V . Broad-billed Sandpiper *Limicola falcinellus*
A V . Stilt Sandpiper *Micropalama himantopus*
A V . Buff-breasted Sandpiper *Tryngites subruficollis*
A P 2 Ruff *Philomachus pugnax*
A W . Jack Snipe *Lymnocryptes minimus*
A R 5 Snipe *Gallinago gallinago*
A V . Great Snipe *G. media*
A V . Short-billed Dowitcher *Limnodromus griseus*
A V . Long-billed Dowitcher *L. scolopaceus*
A R 5 Woodcock *Scolopax rusticola*
A P 2 Black-tailed Godwit *Limosa limosa*
A W . Bar-tailed Godwit *L. lapponica*
B V . Eskimo Curlew *Numenius borealis*
A P 3 Whimbrel *N. phaeopus*
A R 5 Curlew *N. arquata*
A V . Upland Sandpiper *Bartramia longicauda*
A P . Spotted Redshank *Tringa erythropus*
A R 5 Redshank *T. totanus*
A V . Marsh Sandpiper *T. stagnatilis*
A P 3 Greenshank *T. nebularia*
A V . Greater Yellowlegs *T. melanoleuca*
A V . Lesser Yellowlegs *T. flavipes*
A V . Solitary Sandpiper *T. solitaria*
A P 0 Green Sandpiper *T. ochropus*
A P 1 Wood Sandpiper *T. glareola*
A V . Terek Sandpiper *Xenus cinereus*
A S 5 Common Sandpiper *Actitis hypoleucos*
A V 0 Spotted Sandpiper *A. macularia*
A W . Turnstone *Arenaria interpres*
A V . Wilson's Phalarope *Phalaropus tricolor*
A S 2 Red-necked Phalarope *P. lobatus*
A P . Grey Phalarope *P. fulicarius*

STERCORARIIDAE

A P . Pomarine Skua *Stercorarius pomarinus*
A S 4 Arctic Skua *S. parasiticus*

A V . Long-tailed Skua *S. longicaudus*
A S 4 Great Skua *S. skua*

LARIDAE
A V . Great Black-headed Gull *Larus ichthyaetus*
A W 0 Mediterranean Gull *L. melanocephalus*
A V . Laughing Gull *L. atricilla*
A V . Franklin's Gull *L. pipixcan*
A P 0 Little Gull *L. minutus*
A P . Sabine's Gull *L. sabini*
A V . Bonaparte's Gull *L. philadelphia*
A R 6 Black-headed Gull *L. ridibundus*
A V . Slender-billed Gull *L. genei*
A V . Ring-billed Gull *L. delawarensis*
A R 5 Common Gull *L. canus*
A S 5 Lesser Black-backed Gull *L. fuscus*
A R 6 Herring Gull *L. argentatus*
A W . Iceland Gull *L. glaucoides*
A W . Glaucous Gull *L. hyperboreus*
A R 5 Great Black-backed Gull *L. marinus*
A V . Ross's Gull *Rhodostethia rosea*
A S 6 Kittiwake *Rissa tridactyla*
A V . Ivory Gull *Pagophila eburnea*

STERNIDAE
A V 0 Gull-billed Tern *Gelochelidon nilotica*
A V . Caspian Tern *Sterna caspia*
A V . Royal Tern *S. maxima*
A S 5 Sandwich Tern *S. sandvicensis*
A S 4 Roseate Tern *S. dougallii*
A S 5 Common Tern *S. hirundo*
A S 5 Arctic Tern *S. paradisaea*
A V . Bridled Tern *S. anaethetus*
A V . Sooty Tern *S. fuscata*
A S ·4 Little Tern *S. albifrons*
A V . Whiskered Tern *Chlidonias hybridus*
A P 0 Black Tern *C. niger*
A V . White-winged Black Tern *C. leucopterus*

ALCIDAE
A S 6 Guillemot *Uria aalge*
A V . Brünnich's Guillemot *U. lomvia*
A S 6 Razorbill *Alca torda*
B – 0 Great Auk *Pinguinus impennis*
A R 4 Black Guillemot *Cepphus grylle*
A W . Little Auk *Alle alle*
A S 6 Puffin *Fratercula arctica*

PTEROCLIDIDAE
A V 0 Pallas's Sandgrouse *Syrrhaptes paradoxus*

COLUMBIDAE
A R 6 Rock Dove *Columba livia*
A R 6 Stock Dove *C. oenas*
A R 7 Woodpigeon *C. palumbus*
A R 5 Collared Dove *Streptopelia decaocto*
A S 6 Turtle Dove *S. turtur*
A V . Rufous Turtle Dove *S. orientalis*

PSITTACIDAE
D R 1 Ring-necked Parakeet *Psittacula krameri*

CUCULIDAE
A V . Great Spotted Cuckoo *Clamator glandarius*
A S 5 Cuckoo *Cuculus canorus*
A V . Black-billed Cuckoo *Coccyzus erythropthalmus*
A V . Yellow-billed Cuckoo *C. americanus*

TYTONIDAE
A R 4 Barn Owl *Tyto alba*

STRIGIDAE
A V . Scops Owl *Otus scops*
B V . Eagle Owl *Bubo bubo*
A V 0 Snowy Owl *Nyctea scandiaca*
A V . Hawk Owl *Surnia ulula*
A R 4 Little Owl *Athene noctua*
A R 5 Tawny Owl *Strix aluco*
A R 4 Long-eared Owl *Asio otus*
A W 4 Short-eared Owl *A. flammeus*
A V . Tengmalm's Owl *Aegolius funereus*

CAPRIMULGIDAE
A S 4 Nightjar *Caprimulgus europaeus*
B V . Red-necked Nightjar *C. ruficollis*
B V . Egyptian Nightjar *C. aegyptius*
A V . Common Nighthawk *Chordeiles minor*

APODIDAE
A V . Needle-tailed Swift *Hirundapus caudacutus*
A S 5 Swift *Apus apus*
P V . Pallid Swift *A. pallidus*
A V . Alpine Swift *A. melba*
A V . Little Swift *A. affinis*

ALCEDINIDAE
A R 4 Kingfisher *Alcedo atthis*

MEROPIDAE
A V . Blue-cheeked Bee-eater *Merops superciliosus*
A V 0 Bee-eater *M. apiaster*

CORACIIDAE
A V . Roller *Coracias garrulus*

UPUPIDAE
A P 0 Hoopoe *Upupa epops*

PICIDAE
A P 1 Wryneck *Jynx torquilla*
D V . Yellow-shafted Flicker *Colaptes auratus*
A R 5 Green Woodpecker *Picus viridis*
A V . Yellow-bellied Sapsucker *Sphyrapicus varius*
A R 5 Great Spotted Woodpecker *Dendrocopos major*
A R 4 Lesser Spotted Woodpecker *D. minor*

Passeriformes

ALAUDIDAE

A V . Calandra Lark *Melanocorypha calandra*
A V . Bimaculated Lark *M. bimaculata*
A V . White-winged Lark *M. leucoptera*
A V . Short-toed Lark *Calandrella cinerea*
A V . Lesser Short-toed Lark *C. rufescens*
A V . Crested Lark *Galerida cristata*
A R 3 Woodlark *Lullula arborea*
A R 7 Skylark *Alauda arvensis*
A W 0 Shore Lark *Eremophila alpestris*

HIRUNDINIDAE

A S 6 Sand Martin *Riparia riparia*
A S 6 Swallow *Hirundo rustica*
A V . Red-rumped Swallow *H. daurica*
A S 6 House Martin *Delichon urbica*

MOTACILLIDAE

A V . Richard's Pipit *Anthus novaeseelandiae*
A V . Tawny Pipit *A. campestris*
A V . Olive-backed Pipit *A. hodgsoni*
A S 5 Tree Pipit *A. trivialis*
A V . Pechora Pipit *A. gustavi*
A R 7 Meadow Pipit *A. pratensis*
A V . Red-throated Pipit *A. cervinus*
A R 5 Rock Pipit *A. spinoletta*
A S 5 Yellow Wagtail *Motacilla flava*
A V . Citrine Wagtail *M. citreola*
A R 5 Grey Wagtail *M. cinerea*
A R 6 Pied Wagtail *M. alba*

BOMBYCILLIDAE

A W . Waxwing *Bombycilla garrulus*

CINCLIDAE

A R 5 Dipper *Cinclus cinclus*

TROGLODYTIDAE

A R 7 Wren *Troglodytes troglodytes*

MIMIDAE

A V . Brown Thrasher *Toxostoma rufum*

PRUNELLIDAE

A R 7 Dunnock *Prunella modularis*
A V . Alpine Accentor *P. collaris*

TURDIDAE

A V . Rufous Bush Robin *Cercotrichas galactotes*
A R 7 Robin *Erithacus rubecula*
A V . Thrush Nightingale *Luscinia luscinia*
A S 4 Nightingale *L. megarhynchos*
A V . Siberian Rubythroat *L. calliope*
A P 0 Bluethroat *L. svecica*
A V . Red-flanked Bluetail *Tarsiger cyanurus*
A P 2 Black Redstart *Phoenicurus ochruros*

A S 5 Redstart *P. phoenicurus*
A S 5 Whinchat *Saxicola rubetra*
A R 5 Stonechat *S. torquata*
B V . Isabelline Wheatear *Oenanthe isabellina*
A S 5 Wheatear *O. oenanthe*
A V . Pied Wheatear *O. pleschanka*
A V . Black-eared Wheatear *O. hispanica*
A V . Desert Wheatear *O. deserti*
A V . Black Wheatear *O. leucura*
A V . Rock Thrush *Monticola saxatilis*
D V . Blue Rock Thrush *M. solitarius*
A V . White's Thrush *Zoothera dauma*
A V . Siberian Thrush *Z. sibirica*
A V . Hermit Thrush *Catharus guttatus*
A V . Swainson's Thrush *C. ustulatus*
A V . Grey-cheeked Thrush *C. minimus*
A V . Veery *C. fuscescens*
A S 5 Ring Ouzel *Turdus torquatus*
A R 7 Blackbird *T. merula*
A V . Eye-browed Thrush *T. obscurus*
A V . Dusky/Naumann's Thrush *T. naumanni*
A V . Black-throated/Red-throated Thrush *T. ruficollis*
A W 1 Fieldfare *T. pilaris*
A R 7 Song Thrush *T. philomelos*
A W 2 Redwing *T. iliacus*
A R 6 Mistle Thrush *T. viscivorus*
A V . American Robin *T. migratorius*

SYLVIIDAE

A R 3 Cetti's Warbler *Cettia cetti*
A V . Fan-tailed Warbler *Cisticola juncidis*
A V . Pallas's Grasshopper Warbler *Locustella certhiola*
A V . Lanceolated Warbler *L. lanceolata*
A S 5 Grasshopper Warbler *L. naevia*
A V . River Warbler *L. fluviatilis*
A S 1 Savi's Warbler *L. luscinioides*
A V 0 Moustached Warbler *Acrocephalus melanopogon*
A V . Aquatic Warbler *A. paludicola*
A S 6 Sedge Warbler *A. schoenobaenus*
A V . Paddyfield Warbler *A. agricola*
A V . Blyth's Reed Warbler *A. dumetorum*
A S 2 Marsh Warbler *A. palustris*
A S 5 Reed Warbler *A. scirpaceus*
A V . Great Reed Warbler *A. arundinaceus*
A V . Thick-billed Warbler *A. aedon*
A V . Olivaceous Warbler *Hippolais pallida*
A V . Booted Warbler *H. caligata*
A P . Icterine Warbler *H. icterina*
A P . Melodious Warbler *H. polyglotta*
A R 3 Dartford Warbler *Sylvia undata*
A V . Spectacled Warbler *S. conspicillata*
A V . Subalpine Warbler *S. cantillans*
A V . Sardinian Warbler *S. melanocephala*
P V . Rüppell's Warbler *S. rueppelli*
A V . Desert Warbler *S. nana*
A V . Orphean Warbler *S. hortensis*
A P . Barred Warbler *S. nisoria*
A S 5 Lesser Whitethroat *S. curruca*